Building with Straw

Gernot Minke · Friedemann Mahlke

Building with Straw

Design and Technology of a Sustainable Architecture

Birkhäuser – Publishers for Architecture
Basel · Berlin · Boston

Table of contents

I The technology of straw bale building

1 Introduction 9
Purpose and objectives of this book 9
About the contents 9
Building with straw – a contribution to sustainability
  in construction 10
Further advantages of straw bale building 10
Objections and anxieties 11

2 History and proliferation of straw bale building 13
Early buildings (1880 –1970) 13
The development after 1980 15

3 Straw as building material 19
General facts 19
Straw bales 19
Straw panels 20

4 Wall construction systems using straw bales 21
Introduction to the construction systems 21
Load-bearing straw bale walls 22
Non-loadbearing straw bale walls 23
Facing straw bale layer as thermal insulation 23
Structural and dynamic aspects 23
Summary and comparison of the individual systems 24

5 Roof and floor construction with straw bales 25
Roof insulation 25
Floor constructions 26
Supplementary thermal insulation of existing structures 27

6 Physical aspects of straw bale building 28
Heat storage and heat conductivity 28
Thermal bridges 28
Thermal insulation 29
Moisture protection 30
Moisture balance 33
Wind and air tightness 34
Fire protection 34
Sound insulation 35

7 Designing a straw bale building 36
Special aspects of load-bearing straw bale walls 36
Special aspects of non-loadbearing straw bale walls 38
Detailing of foundations 39
Base details 40
Wall build-up 40
Wall junctions with foundation, base and floor 42
Ring beams 43
Windows and doors 44
Wall corners 45
Wall/Roof junctions 45
Interior walls 45
Intermediate ceilings 46
Service ducts 46
Heavy-duty fixings in straw bale walls 46
Wall recesses 46

8 Surface protection and finishing works 48
Interior render 48
Exterior render 49
Paint coats 52
Water-repellent treatment 54
Weather boarding, facing and ventilated cladding 55

9 The building process 56
Supervision and co-ordination on site 56
Health and safety measures 56
Assessment of the quality of the bales 56
Supplementary compaction of the bales 56
Transport and storage 57
Separating of bales 57
Reshaping of bales 58
Bale installation 59
Wall reinforcement 59
Wall prestressing 60
Removal of deformations 61
Back-filling of joints and gaps 62
Cropping of bale surfaces 62
Rendering of the walls 62

10 Trial and error – an example 63
Preliminary note 63
Scheme design 63
Construction – the first attempt 65
Solving the problems – the second attempt 69

11 Building cost, insurance, planning permission 71
Building cost, expenditure of time and personal
contribution 71
Insurance of building 71
Planning permission 72

II Built examples in detail 73

Residences
Residential building in Ouwerkerk, Zeeland, the Nether-
lands 74
Residential building in Balneario Punta Ballena, Uruguay 77
Residential building in central Montreal, Canada 78
Prefabricated single-family home in Hitzendorf, near Graz,
Styria, Austria 80
Single-family home in Dobersdorf, Burgenland, Austria 82
Urban cottage in Berkeley, California, USA 84
Single-family home in Bryson City, North Carolina, USA 86
Single-family home with guest house, games room and
garage in Galston, near Sidney, Australia 88
Single-family home in Lower Lake, California, USA 90
Single-family home at Lake Biwa, Japan 92
The Spiral House, Castlebar, County Mayo, Ireland 94
Load-bearing straw bale house in Disentis, Switzerland 96
Passive house in Cavan, Ontario, Canada 98
First straw bale house in Vienna, Austria 100
Single-family home in Blanden, Belgium 103
Low-energy house in Maria Laach, Austria 104
Passive house in Wienerherberg, Austria 106

Home and workplace
Trout Farm Complex, Tassaraja Canyon, California, USA 108
Residential and office building in London, United Kingdom 110

Ulenkrug Farm, Stubbendorf, Mecklenburg-West Pomerania,
Germany 113
Residential building for ethnic German resettlers,
Wargoldshausen, Lower Franconia, Germany 114
The Woodage Sawmill in Mittagong, Australia 116
Straw bale dome as a rehearsal and performance space
in Forstmehren, Westerwald, Germany 118
Farm and residential building near Rothenburg ob der
Tauber, Franconia, Germany 121
House of a painter near Santa Cruz, California, USA 123

Educational and cultural buildings
Foothills Academy College Preparatory, Scottsdale,
Arizona, USA 125
Real Goods Solar Living Center, Hopland, California,
USA 128
International Sivananda Yoga Vedanta Center Lodge,
Val-Morin, Quebec, Canada 130
Waldorf school in Carbondale, Colorado, USA 132
Salem Children's Village, Kaliningrad, Russia 134
Sanctuary House, Crestone, Colorado, USA 136
Vipassana Meditation Hall, Blackheath, Australia 137

Appendices 138
Measures 138
Networks 139
Internet links 140
Bibliography 142
Acknowledgements 143
Illustration credits 143

I The technology of straw building

1 Introduction

Purpose and objectives of this book

Straw bale building has been experiencing a veritable boom since the 1990s, which first emanated from the USA – here, in fact, an increase in activities showed itself as early as the 1970s – and then spread to Canada and Australia. The renewed interest in straw bale construction also inspired and spurred on those who had been experimenting in this field in Europe, and it is gradually reaching Asia and South America as well.

The idea to use straw as a building material and the know-how of the various techniques that are being used left the ecological domain a long time ago. Increasingly, international and national networks and symposia on this topic are also attracting mainstream architects and engineers. Various examples of completed buildings, among them private residences as well as commercial, educational and cultural buildings, prove the point that straw bale building offers a fresh and highly promising outlook – both from an environmental and an economical perspective.

In contrast to most publications on straw bale building in the past, this book explains in great detail the structural and physical aspects and problems of this building technique. It gives planners and builders – be they architects, engineers, craftsmen or laymen – an idea of the building-physical and structural basics and particularities of straw bale building and highlights potential faults that may lead to avoidable damages. The pictured projects from different countries and climatic zones emphasise the great variety of applications and designs of straw bale building and present this building technique as a sustainable, inexpensive alternative to conventional building methods.

About the contents

The *first chapter* of the book highlights the advantages and disadvantages of straw bale building, particularly with a view to the now common demand for sustainability. It also relates to second thoughts and anxieties of potential users. The *second chapter* contains a brief account of the history of straw bale building and its current state of proliferation. The *third chapter* gives an introduction on the structural and physical properties of straw as building material and straw bales as building elements.

Chapters four to *six* describe different wall construction systems with their respective pros and cons and elaborate the possibilities of insulating roofs and floors with straw bales. This part also touches on the important issues of thermal insulation, fire protection, moisture protection and sound insulation.

The *seventh chapter* deals with those aspects crucial in terms of scheme and detailed design of straw bale houses. Moreover, this part contains drawings of all-important structural details.

The *eighth chapter* draws attention to the

various options of weather proofing and finishing of walls. *Chapters nine* and *ten* describe the procedures on site and give advice on how faults can be avoided. In *chapters 11* to *13*, common planning-related issues such as cost and time planning, insurance, building regulations and the development application procedures are explained.

Finally, *Part II* closes with an assorted selection of modern straw bale houses from all over the world. The book's appendix contains references to related publications and a contact list with addresses where up-to-date information on current projects and research can be retrieved.

left 1.1
below 1.2

Building with straw – a contribution to sustainability in construction

Straw is a renewable building material that will grow again every year. It is a ubiquitous resource that is naturally recyclable and does not pose any problems in terms of its disposal: in the event of building demolition it can be easily separated from other materials and – for instance – can be used as mulch in the garden or in agriculture for the de-compacting of soil. The production of straw bales and transport to the building site consume relatively little energy compared to other building materials; thus, this construction method has hardly any negative impact on the environment. The production of straw bales consumes approximately 14 MJ/m^3 of energy – as opposed to mineral wool, which requires 1,077 MJ/m^3 for its production, 77 times more than straw. The chemical absorption of carbon dioxide during photosynthesis is proportionally even higher than the carbon dioxide emissions caused by the production and transport of straw bales.

Buildings with thermal insulation made of straw can, therefore, help to substantially reduce carbon dioxide emissions in the construction industry. Consequently, straw meets all the requirements of a "sustainable" building material, even more so than

wood since the production and processing of timber require much more energy and produce much more carbon dioxide than the production of straw bales from straw.

1.1 to 1.4
Construction of a straw bale building in Australia during a workshop in 2002

Further advantages of straw bale building

Official building tests on straw bale walls conducted in Germany and Austria produced the following results:

- fire resistance rating of F90
- material designation: normally inflammable
- coefficient of heat conductivity:
  $\lambda_R = 0.0456$ W/mK

This means, that straw bale insulated wall structures can be used for all one- and two-storey buildings, no matter whether they are single-family or duplex homes, terrace houses, garages, agricultural buildings, childcare centres, schools, hospitals or office buildings. Under certain conditions, multistorey buildings can be also permissible (refer to Part II).

Straw bale insulated houses can achieve passive-house standards. Passive houses are buildings with an annual heating energy consumption of less than 15 kWh/m². In

1.3

such buildings the installation of a conventional heating system is not economical as the heating cost is lower than the standing charge for a gas connection, possibly even lower than the cost for the operation of the circulation pump of a conventional heating system.

In Germany's agricultural production, for instance, straw is available in large quantities. According to Scharmer, the amount produced annually would be sufficient to insulate about 350,000 single-family homes (Scharmer 2002). Whereas straw is nowadays mainly pressed in round bales, there are still sufficient numbers of unused small

1.4

bale presses around on local farms, which could serve for the production of the required reshaped bales.

The long lifespan of straw bale buildings is proven by numerous examples from the United States. The oldest still inhabited house is approximately 100 years old (refer to chapter two).

Straw bales are ideal for do-it-yourself construction: the advantages do not only encompass building-cost savings, but also the social interaction of the participants of the building process. Family members, neighbours and friends that are usually excluded from the building process can participate. This creates a strong sense of identity for the clients and possibly their children with their own house, their "own four walls." For all participants, the act of the house building is an exciting interactive and gratifying social experience. In the USA, Canada and Australia, the future house owners will frequently host so-called "work parties" to raise the straw bale walls, inviting friends and family and even strangers to join them. Images 1.1 to 1.4 show the construction of a straw bale building as part of an international conference in Australia with straw bale builders from all over the world.

Objections and anxieties

Frequently, one stumbles across substantial doubts and subliminal anxiety when people are confronted with the idea of living or working in houses with walls made of straw bales. These reactions are mainly due to a lack of knowledge and an irrational fear of the new and unknown. This book will try to face the lack of knowledge by enlightening the reader through competent information; the mentioned anxiety can only be dispersed by means of rational arguments – another task this book will attempt to tackle.

In the USA, research has repeatedly addressed the issue of whether insects, mice or even rats lived in historical straw bale buildings – which was, however, not the case. Even in a test building that was dismantled after four years and where every single straw bale was examined, no evidence of the existence of vermin could be found (http://swarthmore.edu/es/straw-bale.html).

Fire hazard

No one would deny the fact that loose straw easily catches fire; however, the reality that straw bale walls that are rendered on both sides achieve a fire resistance of 90 minutes (F90 rating) is still widely unknown. This was first established according to Austrian building standards (refer to chapter six) and has meanwhile also been verified in Germany.

A nesting site for mice

Mice do not feed on straw and the highly pressed straw bales with a density of 90 kg/m^3 and more are strong enough to resist any rodent's onslaught. A potential risk are cavities between the bales that have not, or not sufficiently, been stuffed. However, as the walls are rendered, mice would have to penetrate a 3- to 6-cm-strong layer of plaster, which has not been observed as yet. If the exterior weather protection consists of a ventilated rain-screen timber cladding instead of render, it is theoretically conceivable that mice might nest in the cavity – as might be the case with any other ventilated exterior cladding as well. However, this has never been observed, either, since these cavities would be too cold in winter when mice are attracted by the warmth of houses. In addition, German building regulations stipulate that such cavities be closed with insect meshes in order to prevent wasps and hornets from nesting there.

Termites

Evidently, straw is not a feast for termites either. Some species may be able to digest straw, but they clearly prefer wood as food. Steen et al. report that doors and window frames of a historical straw bale house were infested – the straw itself, however, remained intact (Steen et al. 1994, page 64).

Moulds

The fear that moulds might develop on straw bales is unfounded – provided the correct construction rules are observed; moulds cannot develop on dry straw. The correct construction rules involve the use of dry straw bales; that means that their moisture content is lower than 15 %, and that either a vapour barrier is installed on the inside surface to prevent moisture from entering the bales or that the exterior finish is vapour-permeable enough so that potential condensate can diffuse out. Whether or not a wall build-up complies with these requirements can be established by means of officially authorised methods of calculation (refer to chapter six).

During plastering, it has to be made sure that the plaster dries out relatively fast. For this, the plaster must allow sufficient diffusion so that the straw, which has become moist during plastering, can dry out quickly. If the earth plaster contains too many organic aggregates such as sawdust or straw chaff, it will dry out very slowly, which facilitates the formation of moulds. Hence, builders have to make sure – especially when the plaster layers are thick – that the earlier layers dry out before the last layer is applied. Furthermore, the last layer should contain no – or at least very few – organic additives.

According to Viitanen (1996), the ideal environment for the development of moulds are temperatures of about 20 to 28 °C and a relative air humidity of more than 55 %. Other sources state values of over 80 to 90 %.

Dust allergies

As a result of the building process, people with dust allergies may be affected and face unpleasant consequences. Allergic persons should therefore wear a breathing protection mask as a precaution. Occupants of a completed building with rendered walls will not face any risk.

Note

For the conversion of metric values into imperial ones, see page 138.

2 History and proliferation of straw bale building

above 2.1
Fawn Lake Ranch,
Hyannis, Nebraska,
1900–1914
right 2.2 Martin Mon-
hart House, Arthur,
Nebraska, 1925

Early buildings (1880–1970)

The beginning of the history of straw bale building coincides with the appearance of straw bale presses in the USA in the 19th century: in 1872, a horse power driven press is mentioned, by 1884, there were steam-driven presses. The first recorded straw bale buildings were erected in Nebraska. By 1886, a school with a single class room had been built near Bayard, Scott's Bluff County (Steen et al. 1994). These early straw bale build-ings were constructed without timber substructure, with the straw bale walls directly supporting the roof. In the literature, this "load-bearing" construction method was later called "Nebraska technique."
The oldest remaining straw bale buildings erected with the load-bearing method that are still inhabited were built between 1900 and 1914 and were extended in 1940 (*2.1*). In 1903, the Burke House was built in Alliance, Nebraska, and has been unoccupied since 1956 (*2.3*). The technique had its heyday between 1915 and 1930; Welsch (1970) mentions approximately 70 buildings from this period, 13 of which survived after 1993.
A church with load-bearing straw bale walls, the Pilgrim Holiness Church, was built in Arthur, Nebraska, in 1928 (*2.4*). The oldest known straw bale building of Europe – and probably the oldest two-storey straw bale insulated building worldwide – is "Maison Feuillette", built in 1921 in Montargis, France, (*2.5*). This 100-m² house meanwhile accom-

modates the third generation (Wedig 1999). Burrit Mansion in Huntsville, Alabama, (*2.7*) was built in 1938 and is probably one of the first wooden two-storey post-and-beam structures with straw bale infill panels in the USA; it contains 2,200 straw bales as part of its walls, ceilings and roof. Today, it is a museum. Arguably the oldest straw bale building in the Netherlands is the house in Heeze (*2.6*), which was built in 1944 (Steen et al. 1994).

right 2.3 Burk House,
Nebraska, USA, 1903
below 2.6 Neeze
Country House , the
Netherlands, 1944

left 2.4 Pilgrim Holi-
ness Church, Arthur,
Nebraska, 1928
below 2.7 Burrit Man-
sion, Huntsville, Alaba-
ma, USA, 1938

above 2.5 Maison
Feuillette, Montargis,
France, 1921

The development after 1980

The 1970s and 1980s produced a fair number of publications on the topic in the USA, adding to the renaissance of straw bale building. They advocated both the load-bearing Nebraska technique and the use of straw bales as infill panels in timber constructions (Welsch 1973; Doolittle 1973; McElderry 1979; Strang 1983).

Since 1993, there is the quarterly magazine "The Last Straw – The Journal of Straw Bale Construction" (*2.8*). The subsequent sudden boom of straw bale building caused various states to enact specific building regulations (refer to chapter 13). The first official directives in the USA were the "New Mexico Straw-Bale Construction Guidelines" of 1991. In the 1990s, extensive research was conducted throughout the USA to establish reliable performance data on thermal insulation, load-bearing capacity, wind and earthquake resistance as well as behaviour in fire (King 1996). In the 1980s, the first workshops for the experimental construction of buildings had been carried out, first in the USA, later also in Canada and England.

In the beginning of the 1990s, there was a downright straw bale boom in the USA, mainly consisting in do-it-yourself building activities. In 1991, authorities granted the first official planning permissions and banks financed straw bale buildings in New Mexico and soon elsewhere.

The first international conference on straw bale building was held in 1993 and led to the foundation of the National Straw Bale Research Advisory Network. Meanwhile, many more national networks for the proliferation of straw bale building were created, for instance the German association of straw builders, *Fachverband Strohballenbau,* founded in 2002 (for addresses, refer to page 139 and 140). Meanwhile, in the USA, Canada, Australia, England and Austria, there are also professional contractors specialising in the erection of straw bale buildings.

right 2.10 Load-bearing show building for "Green Week", Brussels 2002 (Harald Wedig, André de Bonter)

above 2.9 Test building, Recklinghausen 1997 (Martin Oehlmann, Harald Wedig)

right 2.8 Cover of the "The Last Straw" magazine

Whereas many European countries hosted specific workshops in the 1990s, in Germany the development started relatively late: the first seminar was held in Pommritz in 1995 by Martin Oehlmann and Harald Wedig. As a result, a little garden house was

constructed. Image *2.9* shows the building that was erected in 1997 as part of the second workshop in Recklinghausen, Germany. Among the pioneers of straw bale workshops in the USA were Matts Myhrmann, Judy Knox, Bill and Athena Steen, David Eisenberg and Steve McDonald; in Europe they were Rolf Brinkmann, Martin Oehlmann and Harald Wedig.

As part of the European Union's "Green Week", the "Global Ecovillage Network" under the guidance of Harald Wedig erect-

right 2.12 Two-storey, load-bearing residential building, Ireland (Barbara Jones), 2000

from left to right
2.13 Residential building in Norway (Arild Berg/Rolf Jacobson)
2.11 Residential building in Brittany (Pascal Thepaut), "Gagné technique"
2.14 Hospital, Mongolia 2002 (Tsagaan Delger)

ed a show house on the square in front of the European Commission in Brussels (*2.10*), which was subsequently dismantled and now stands in a natural reserve near Viersen, Germany.

The first commercially constructed load-bearing straw bale buildings in Europe were built in England starting from 1989. Whereas in 1995 there were about 40 straw bale buildings in England, Norway and France, this number had already increased to about 400 in Europe by 2001. In France, straw bale buildings were predominantly erected in Brittany (*2.11*). In 1998, Brittany also hosted the first International Straw Construction Meeting in Europe, and in the same year a Straw Construction Symposium was held in the Netherlands. Also in the same year, the first building permissions were granted there for two straw bale houses.

In 1998, Barbara Jones built the first two-storey load-bearing house (2.12) in Ireland. In Switzerland in 1999, Ruedi Kunz erected a hybrid (load-bearing and post-and-beam) structure with a compass roof that had received planning consent. Norway counted already more than 25 buildings before the end of the 20th century, most of them by Rolf Jacobson (*2.13*). In Belarus, a straw bale settlement built for Chernobyl refugees received the World Sustainable Energy Award in 2000. Altogether, approximately 200 government-sponsored houses were erected there (Wedig 1999). In the High Tatras in Slovakia, Windrose Co planned 100 straw bale buildings; and in Mongolia, more than 100 buildings made of straw bales have been built as part of a UN programme since 1997 (Gruber, Gruber 2000) (*2.14*). Even before modern straw bale building became successful in the USA during the 1980s and a long time before it reached Europe, the German architect Rudolf Doernach built a wooden post-and-beam structure consisting of round timber posts and straw bale insulated walls in Hennef-

left 2.16 Windeck Werfen, first straw bale building erected with building permission in Germany (Ruth and Matthias Bönisch), 1999
below right 2.17 Studio building Guhreitzen (Dirk Scharmer), 2000

above 2.15 Biohaus Süchterscheid, 1979 (Rudolf Doernach)
right 2.18 Residential building for ethnic German resettlers in Wargoldshausen, Lower Franconia (Achim Wüst), 2001

above 2.19 Residential settlement Sieben Linden, Wendland, 2004

2.20 Winery and storage building, Lethbridge, Australia, 1999

Süchterscheid in 1979 (*2.15*). However, the building did not receive wide attention and remained unknown to the international alternative building community. Possibly, that was due to the fact that the building was based on a somewhat immature design: bales were not plastered but covered only by a rough exterior timber cladding. In order to achieve wind-tightness, the bales were covered with foil on the outside. That, however, obstructed vapour diffusion – thus leading to partial decay. Consequently, the bales had to be removed a few years later and were replaced with a conventional wall build-up.

After that, no further straw bale buildings were built in Germany for almost 20 years. Only since 1995 have some small experimental structures been built as part of seminars guided by Martin Oehlmann, Harald Wedig, Rolf Brinkmann and others. The first straw bale building with planning consent was built in 1999 by architect *Matthias Bönisch* (*2.16*). Further projects were to follow, for instance the studio building in Guhreitzen, planned and built by Dirk Scharmer and erected with Jumbo bales

(*2.17*), or a two-storey residential building for ethnic German resettlers in Bavaria (*2.18*). A rather exceptional project is the community building that is currently being built in an eco village in the German Wendland area: it is being erected without the aid of power tools and largely renounces conventional building materials (*2.19*).

Whereas in Germany straw bale buildings have so far only been permitted as wooden post-and-beam structures with straw bale infill panels, in countries like Canada, Ireland and Switzerland even two-storey buildings with load-bearing straw bale walls have received planning permission by local authorities (refer to Part II). One of the largest load-bearing straw bale buildings was erected in 1998 in Lethbridge, Australia (*2.20*): it is a 250-m^2 winery building with storage and vending facilities; the 4.6-m-tall walls are made of 220 Jumbo bales of 90 cm x 90 cm x 240 cm. The bales have a weight of about 225 kg and were erected with the help of a front loader in three days (Goodwin 2000).

3 Straw as a building material

General facts

The term straw denotes the dry stems of threshed grain (wheat, rye, barley, oats, millet) or fibrous plants (flax, hemp, rice) – or more precisely: the part between root stem and ear. Straw is a regenerative resource that develops out of photosynthesis using solar energy, water and minerals in the ground. It consists of cellulose, lignin and silica and possesses a waxy, water-repellent skin. Most suitable for the production of bales for building is wheat, spelt and rye straw – as opposed to barley and oats which are less stable.

Due to its high silica content, straw rots extremely slowly. In agriculture it is, therefore, frequently used for the de-compacting of soil, as ground cover in stables or as a fodder additive in winter. Only rarely is straw used as fuel or for the production of straw panels (refer to this chapter page 20). For centuries, straw was used throughout Europe to thatch roofs (although it should be mentioned here that reed is more suit-

able since it is more durable). As an aggregate to the building material clay it has been used for millennia to increase thermal insulation and reduced the risk of crack formation during drying of the material (for further information, see Minke 2000, chapters 4.7.2, 9.2 and 10.3).

Straw bales

Dimensions

Straw bales are produced in various formats: small bales usually are 32 to 35 cm x 50 cm x 50 cm to 120 cm (occasionally the width of 50 cm can be slightly smaller). The density varies between 80 to 120 kg/m³ (bales with a lower density are not suitable for straw bale building). However, most producers of bale presses have stopped making small versions of their machines.

Width and height of the bales are determined by the cross-sectional measurements of the bale press channel that can be adjusted slightly to produce smaller dimensions. The common length of small straw bales is 80 or 90 cm. Usually, they come in lengths varying from 50 to 100 cm, sometimes even 120 cm, in adjustable steps of about 10 cm: this is due to the fact that the press produces individual layers of straw – of about 10 cm each – which are then tied together with two strings (3.1).

Medium bales with dimensions of 50 cm x 80 cm x 70 to 240 cm and Jumbo bales of 70 cm x 120 cm x 100 to 300 cm or more

3.1 Straw bale dimensions (Lacinski, Bergeron, 2000)

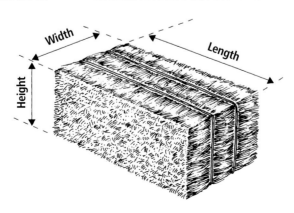

left 3.2 Production of
small bales
below 3.3 Straw panel

are usually only used for load-bearing structures; they result in very large wall thickness and – due to their heavy weight – can only be moved by lifting devices. Their density varies between 180 and 200 kg/m³.

In Australia, two warehouses were built with Jumbo bales in 1998 (see *2.20*). In Trier-Irsch in Germany, an experimental building was begun in 2002 using 90-cm-tall bales that are 1.25 m wide and 2.50 m long and weigh up to 400 kg. In case small bales cannot be sourced locally and if long-distance transport would increase cost significantly, it would also be feasible to unroll existing round bales and press the received mats into small bales.

Things to be observed

Fresh bales of the same harvest often differ in terms of moisture content since the straw is usually damper in the morning than in the late afternoon. For use as a building material the moisture content has to be below 15 %. Furthermore, density and accuracy of shape can vary slightly: the greater the pace of the harvest process, the less accurate is the shape of the bales.

A further compromising factor for the quality of the bales may be the amount of weeds growing on the respective field: weeds are less stable and will decay faster when damp. Straw bales determined for construction use should, therefore, contain no weeds, possess a density of more than 90 kg/m³ and have accurate dimensions.

Stored straw bales should not show any signs of decay or moulds whatsoever; the tying strings should be tight: polypropylene straps are very suitable whereas sisal is too slack.

Straw bales have to be stored in a dry environment, that is, they must not touch moist ground directly and must be protected from rain. On site they are best stored on pallets. Damp bales should be spaced so that they can dry more quickly and do not run the risk of being damaged by micro-organisms.

Straw panels

There are various straw panel products on the market that are produced without the use of glue. Already in the 1920s, straw panels were produced in Switzerland and in France by the trade name of *Solomite*; these were tied together with wire. The English *Stramit* panels are used in constructions throughout the world. The panels are pressed under use of heat and without additional binding agents and are coated with cardboard. They are used as thermal insulation, plaster base or partitions and come in dimensions of 1.20 m x 3.60 m. The German company *Karphos* also produces straw panels without additional binding agents at thicknesses of up to 20 cm. There are also strongly pressed, synthetic resin-glued panels available that have the same strength as chipboard panels.

4 Wall construction systems using straw bales

Introduction to the construction systems

There are two substantially different construction systems:

the load-bearing straw bale wall where the roof loads are transmitted into the foundation directly via the straw bales (*4.1*) and a frame structure, usually consisting of timber posts and beams with straw infill panels or face straw bales (*4.2*). In the literature, the load-bearing system is frequently called "Nebraska technique" due to its invention in Nebraska in the late 19th century.

The frame structure – commonly known as non-loadbearing or infill bale walls – consists of a timber, steel or reinforced concrete frame transmitting the roof loads and stabilising the wall; here, the straw bales have no structural purpose and exclusively serve for thermal insulation.

In 1982, the Canadian Louis Gagné developed a load-bearing wall system (mortared bale matrix system), also known as "Gagné technique": the bales are laid like bricks on cement mortar forming cross-joints. The resulting pattern of vertical and horizontal joints performs – fully or partially – the load-bearing task (*4.3*). This is, therefore, a hybrid system with the straw bales partially performing load-bearing tasks and partially only functioning as infill panels. This system, however, entails the formation of thermal bridges and is consequently not suitable for colder climates – which is why this book will not deal with it in great detail.

Further examples of load-bearing systems are the North-American *Paillobloc System*, *Baleblock System* and *Bioblock*: here, the straw is subjected to high pressure and coated with mortar creating accurate, sharp-edged blocks that are laid with or without mortar bond (Ladinsky, Bergeron, 2000). Again, these systems are not suitable for use in Northern and Central Europe due to thermal bridges.

Another kind of use for straw bales is the supplementary facing of existing walls with straw bales acting as an exterior thermal insulation layer.

In historical buildings, often a mix of different systems can be found within the same

4.1 Load-bearing straw bale wall system

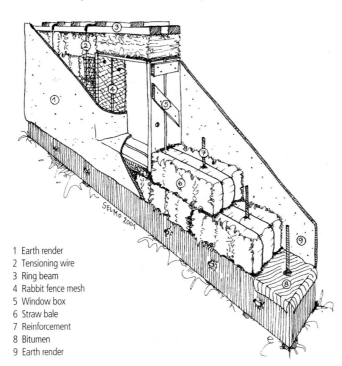

1 Earth render
2 Tensioning wire
3 Ring beam
4 Rabbit fence mesh
5 Window box
6 Straw bale
7 Reinforcement
8 Bitumen
9 Earth render

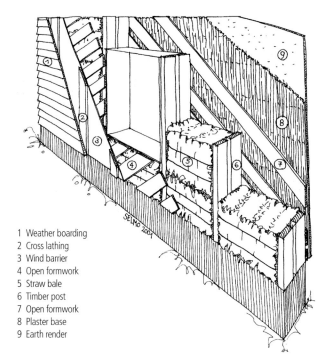

4.2 Non-loadbearing
straw bale wall system

1 Weather boarding
2 Cross lathing
3 Wind barrier
4 Open formwork
5 Straw bale
6 Timber post
7 Open formwork
8 Plaster base
9 Earth render

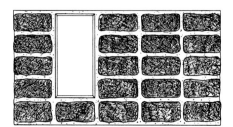

4.3 Gagné system
(Steen et al. 1994)

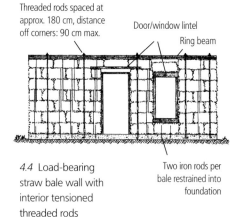

Threaded rods spaced at
approx. 180 cm, distance
off corners: 90 cm max.

Door/window lintel

Ring beam

4.4 Load-bearing
straw bale wall with
interior tensioned
threaded rods

Two iron rods per
bale restrained into
foundation

structure: this frequently leads to problems as load-bearing and non-loadbearing systems tend to have a different behaviour in terms of creeping as well as a different flexibility.

Load-bearing straw bale walls

Walls made out of stacked straw bales, which transmit the roof loads directly into the foundations, are so compelling because of their structural simplicity and the short construction time and low cost, respectively. Therefore, they proliferated quickly throughout the USA after the invention of straw bale presses in the late 19th century (refer to chapter two/page 13).

Although no one will dispute time and cost savings even today, the issue of planning permission remains a problem in Germany – especially as not a single load-bearing straw bale building with official planning permission has been built in Germany as yet. This contrasts with the situation in Switzerland and Austria where planning permissions have already been granted for single- and two-storey buildings of that type (refer to Part II).

By and large, design of load-bearing straw bale buildings is restricted to single-storey buildings. This is down to the fact that the ratio of wall height to wall thickness should not exceed 5:1, which can only be achieved with small bales (all two-storey load-bearing buildings were erected with Jumbo bales). Further restrictions and design criteria will be explained in chapter seven.

An essential requirement for load-bearing walls is that bales are relatively well compressed and that walls are prestressed. To achieve this, a ring beam on top is required, which is then connected to the foundation with tension ties. The prestress of the tension ties inside the wall should ideally be slightly higher than the roof loads so the bales will not receive further compression. The prestress can be created with rods threaded through the centre of the bales or interior and exterior tensioned straps (4.4 and 4.5). If tensioned rods are used they have to be threaded in through the bales, which is time-consuming and requires the rods to be segmented. Therefore, this technique is hardly ever used these days.

A simpler method involves tensioned straps, although here well-balanced prestressing can be difficult and the straps might hamper finishing works.

The Canadian-based company Fibre House Ltd. and Huff 'n' Puff Strawbale Constructions, Australia, developed a system for equal wall prestressing: an inflatable coated

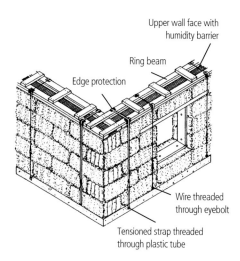

Upper wall face with
humidity barrier

Ring beam

Edge protection

Wire threaded
through eyebolt

Tensioned strap threaded
through plastic tube

fabric tube with a diameter of 20 to 30 cm is installed above the ring beam, compressing the wall by up to 15 cm. However, this method did not prove worthwhile since it is expensive and complicated.

Research conducted on cement-rendered load-bearing walls established that the cement render contributed to the load-bearing capacity of the wall (Lacinski, Bergeron 2000).

Non-loadbearing straw bale walls

In non-loadbearing straw bale walls, frames (usually made of timber posts or studs) perform the structural task rather than the straw bales (*4.6*). The bales function as thermal insulation and usually also as exterior envelope. They can be either placed between the posts as infill panels or as an interior or exterior facing layer. Illustration *4.7* pictures five different options.

In any event, the bales need to be tied to the primary frame structure. If they are not prestressed and tied to the ground they will have to be fixed to each other to create sufficient rigidity to withstand horizontal loads such as wind. (refer to chapter seven/ page 38).

Facing straw bale layer as thermal insulation

For old, poorly insulated buildings, the supplementary addition of a continuous insulating envelope of straw bales is sometimes a cost-efficient and energy-saving solution. The bales have to be either firmly fixed to the existing wall or have to be supported by a secondary framework. The latter has the advantage that it can equally serve as a substructure for a ventilated exterior cladding. However, this can be a fire hazard: even if building regulations do not stipulate it – the exterior face of the bales should always receive at least one layer of plaster, which has to be smoothed out and cover the straw stalks sufficiently so that they do not pose a fire threat.

This solution, on the other hand, has structural disadvantages: in order to accommodate the increased wall thickness and additional loads of the straw bale layer, the foundations may have to be widened or fitted with additional consoles; embrasures will become deeper and the eaves will usually have to be moved out.

Structural and dynamic aspects

The test building described in chapter ten proves the fact that straw bale walls can support roof loads of more than 500 kg per meter wall length (which equals approx. 1,000 kg/m^2). The Californian Straw Bale Code stipulates a maximum vertical load at the top end of the wall of 400 lb/ft^2 = 1,953 kg/m^2 (King 1996, page 142 et seqq.) Surely, straw bale walls can accept higher loads if they are stabilised against buckling. This is achieved by means of the mentioned horizontal and vertical bracing as well as prestressing elements such as threaded rods and straps, which are explained in more in detail in chapter nine. Straw bale walls that are not prestressed tend to buckle quite easily if subjected to horizontal loads such as wind, mechanical impact or earthquakes. This is especially the case if neighbouring

Vertically aligned windows

Window substructure

Load-bearing timber structure

Facing straw bale insulation in front of the timber structure

above 4.6 Framed structure with facing straw bale layer (Lacinski, Bergeron, 2000)
below 4.7 Different possible positions of straw bales and frame structure

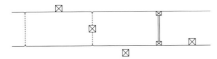

right 4.8 Deformation of loaded straw bales (official testing laboratory for building materials at Trier University of Applied Sciences)
left page 4.5 Load-bearing straw bale wall with exterior tensioned straps (Steen et al. 1994)

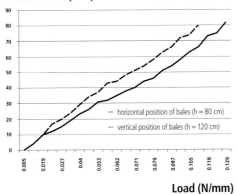

Deformation (mm)

— horizontal position of bales (h = 80 cm)
-- vertical position of bales (h = 120 cm)

Load (N/mm)

bales lack connecting rods, bars or equivalent measures.

When subjected to static loads, straw bales show signs of compression. This will increase, the lower the density of the bales is and the higher the load is. The official testing laboratory for building materials at the University of Applied Sciences in Trier established the deformations shown in figure *4.8* after testing Jumbo bales of 80 cm x 120 cm x 250 cm and a specific weight of 130 kg/m^3. They show that a horizontally positioned bale will be compressed by only 1.25 % when subjected to a load of 2,000 kg/m^2 (20 kN/m^2) and by 5 % when subjected to a load of 7,100 kg/m^2 (71 kN/m^2). This means that compression and load increase are proportional. Deformation of bales is largely elastic: tests in the USA established that when the load on the bales is relieved they will take on their former shape. According to King (1996), the modulus of elasticity varies around 150 psi (1.0 N/mm^2).

Due to their high ductility, straw bale walls provide a relatively good earthquake protection – that is, because of their elasticity they will absorb the kinetic energy of the seismic shocks.

Summary and comparison of the individual systems

– Load-bearing straw bale wall structures are by far more economical than non-loadbearing structures.
– They can be erected much faster and require fewer planning efforts and less trade skills for construction.
– They are the prototype of straw bale building.

The problem of this building method in Germany and some other countries is the lack of authorisation by local planning authorities, although it has been tried and tested for more than 100 years in the USA and has meanwhile been used for buildings with planning permission in Denmark, France, Great Britain, Holland, Ireland, Austria and Switzerland. No evidence against its stability, fire resistance or durability could be produced.

The types of load-bearing structures that have been built in the USA and Canada with vertical and horizontal mortar joints (also see chapter four), are not suitable for North and Central European climates due to the formation of thermal bridges.

As far as the non-loadbearing systems – with straw bales used as facing insulation layer or infill panels – are concerned, they boast the advantage of low cost and excellent thermal insulation – these systems, on the other hand, face disadvantages because of the need for wider foundations, deeper embrasures and greater roof overhangs. Whether such a straw bale house is more economical than a conventionally insulated building cannot be answered with a clear yes or no; the answer will depend on planning, site organisation and many other factors.

The unambiguous advantages are the environmental benefits: straw is a material that does not produce any carbon dioxide or other environmentally toxic emissions during production but – on the contrary – absorbs carbon dioxide from the air during photosynthesis. Another advantage is the fact that straw bales are inexpensive and can be used for do-it-yourself construction, which usually leads to cost savings. Furthermore, straw bale insulated buildings can achieve passive house standard (also see chapter six).

5 Roof and floor construction with straw bales

Roof insulation

Thermal insulation of roofs with straw bales is – in most cases – only economically viable if it is thoroughly considered at planning stage: if the height of the rafters equals the height of bales (approx. 35 cm) and the distance between rafters equals the length of bales, a very simple installation can be achieved. The coefficient of thermal conductivity (or U-value) of this roof build-up is U = 0.14 to 0.16 W/m²K (R-value = 7.1 to 6.2), which meets the standard for low-energy buildings.

5.1 Roof build-up with straw bales between rafters, boarding with vapour barrier

Bituminous fibre board
Straw bales between rafters
Vapour barrier
Timber boarding

5.2 Roof build-up with straw bales between rafters, OSB boarding as vapour barrier

Bituminous fibre board
Straw bales between timber girders
OSB board
Plasterboard

As shown in figure *5.1*, the typical roof build-up consists of a panelling below the rafters with a vapour barrier, for example a Polyethylene (PE) foil on top; at the same time, the foil prevents straw particles from floating down through the panelling joints. If the boarding consists of OSB panels, the construction can do without a vapour barrier – provided all joints are vapour-sealed – since OSB boards possess a high resistance to water vapour diffusion (*5.2*).

In order to achieve a fire-retardant structure (with an F30 fire rating), an additional 12.5-mm fibre cement sheet or plasterboard has to fixed to the soffit.

Rafters can be dimensioned more economically when straw poles are installed on top of them (refer to *5.3*). In this case, the rafters can be covered with tongue-and-groove boarding plus vapour barrier or OSB boards as well.

If the bales are positioned above the primary roof structure, the roof membrane – the weather proof layer, that is – needs to be secured against uplift by wind forces. An additional problem with pitched roofs is the fact that bales tend to slide down leaving a gap at ridge level: therefore, they have to be packed tightly during installation.

While the described roof build-up with a covering of roof tiles, metal sheet or asphalt roofing felt requires a rigid substructure, this is not necessary for a green roof with a sufficiently thick substratum layer (*5.3*). In such an event, the water- and root-proof barrier membrane can be laid directly onto the

5.3 Roof build-up
with straw bales
above rafters, green
roof

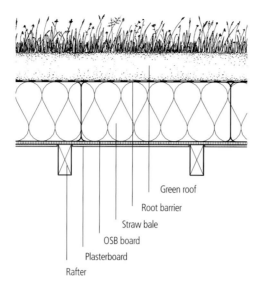

Green roof
Root barrier
Straw bale
OSB board
Plasterboard
Rafter

5.4 Roof build-up
with green roof with-
out roof membrane

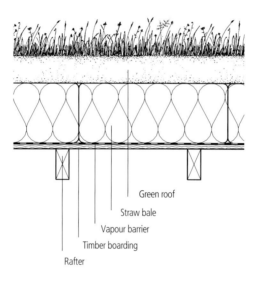

Green roof
Straw bale
Vapour barrier
Timber boarding
Rafter

5.5 Structurally
detached straw bale
layer

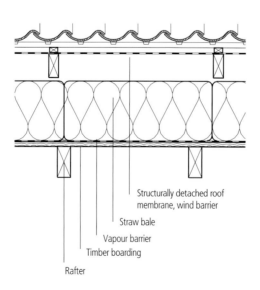

Structurally detached roof
membrane, wind barrier
Straw bale
Vapour barrier
Timber boarding
Rafter

straw bales. Another conceivable solution
is to cover the bales directly with the green
roof layer (*5.4*), which is very inexpensive.
However, in this scenario the straw bales
will sooner or later decay since they have
direct contact with the soil, and moisture
can penetrate them. Although this process
may take many years, the increased moisture content and progressing decay will
significantly diminish the thermal insulation
effect. Therefore, this solution is only suitable for temporary buildings.

Another structural solution is shown in figure *5.5*: the lower roof structure only supports the straw bales and the primary roof
structure receiving wind and snow loads is
structurally detached from it.

For any kind of structural solution it is
advantageous if the bales are ventilated
to enable the drying out of moisture rem-
nants or condensate that might develop
due to a faulty vapour barrier.

Floor constructions

Besides conventional floor construction
methods, straw bales have repeatedly been
used for the insulation of floors in straw
bale buildings. When installed in floor constructions, it has to be made sure that
moisture cannot enter the bales from the
ground and that bales are completely dry.
It is also essential to install a continuous
vapour barrier on top of the bales to prevent the formation of condensate.

A secure method to avoid damages caused
by moisture is to elevate the floor and to
ventilate the space underneath the bales
(refer to *5.6* and *5.7*).

Arguably the most economical solution has
been chosen for the test building discussed
in chapter ten: here, an approximately
10-cm-strong layer of gravel was applied
directly to the ground, then covered with an
about 3-cm-strong layer of sand and a PE
moisture barrier. Recycled timber pallets
serve as ventilated substructure for the
straw bales; floating 24-mm OSB boards
were laid – without additional battens –

directly onto the bales and the joints were sealed with 25-mm-wide screwed-on OSB strips.

Illustration 5.8 shows a similarly inexpensive floor construction suitable for do-it-yourself construction: the straw bales rest on pallets that in turn rest on used car tyres to keep out moisture and create ventilation underneath. This construction does without a moisture barrier.

Supplementary thermal insulation of existing structures

Roof insulation

The supplementary insulation of roofs with straw bales is relatively laborious. The following three solutions are possible:

above 5.8 Economical floor construction with pallets and used tyres

right 5.6 Ventilated floor construction

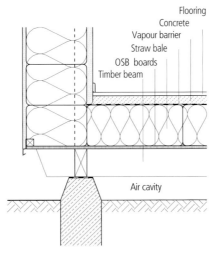

Flooring
Concrete
Vapour barrier
Straw bale
OSB boards
Timber beam

Air cavity

right 5.7 Ventilated floor construction

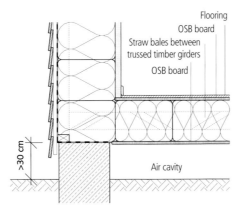

Flooring
OSB board
Straw bales between trussed timber girders
OSB board

>30 cm

Air cavity

Interior insulation

Here, the straw bales are fixed to the existing roof structure from below. Usually they need to be protected by a vapour barrier to avoid contact with condensate.

Exterior insulation, increase in height of roof structure

If the straw bales are to serve as exterior thermal insulation the roofing has to be removed and the height of the roof structure has to be extended to suit the thickness of the bales (approx. 35 cm, *5.1*).

Exterior insulation, floating green roof

If the supplementary insulation with straw bales is topped by a green roof the existing roof structure might not have to be increased in height and the existing roof membrane might be retained – provided the green roof installation follows building regulations; in particular, the roof has to be secured against partial uplift by wind forces. If the roof membrane consists of asphalt roofing felt or another vapour-proof membrane, installation of a vapour barrier below is not required either.

All three solutions have to make sure that no thermal bridges will be formed and no water vapour will enter the bales.

Floor insulation

The supplementary straw bale insulation of floors requires the bales to be protected against penetration of humidity from above as well as from below. The disadvantage of this method is that the room height is reduced and, most importantly, that the doorways will have to be increased in height. Furthermore, a rigid substructure for the flooring is required, which can span freely from wall to wall or float on the lower bales.

6 Physical aspects of straw bale building

Heat storage and heat conductivity

Buildings with sufficient thermal mass provide a balanced and, therefore, comfortable indoor climate. As straw bales have a low (thermal) mass and therefore a poor heat storage capability, the interior finish material of the walls is all-important: A favourable material is earth plaster with a high content of sand and fine gravel. With their high density of 1,900 to 2,100 kg/m^3 these plasters with a thickness of 3 to 6 cm play an important part for the temperature balance of the building. It is also favourable if the interior walls consist of 11.5-cm-thick clay, brick or sand-lime masonry. Earth bricks – and to lesser degree also earth plasters – are also advantageous for the regulation of indoor air-humidity (refer to this chapter page 33). The heat required to warm 1 kg of a substance by one degree in temperature is called *specific heat capacity c*. The specific heat capacity of straw is c = 2.0 KJ/kgK; that of earth is c = 1.0 KJ/kgK.

The heat storage capacity of a building material is determined by the *volume-specific heat capacity S*, which specifies the heat required to warm 1 m^3 of a substance by one degree in temperature:

$$S = c \cdot \rho \ [kJ/m^3K] \text{ or } [Wh/m^3K]$$

The *thermal storage* properties Q_s per unit area of wall is determined by the volume-specific heat capacity S and the thickness s of the building element:

$$Q_s = c \cdot \rho \cdot s \ [kJ/m^2K] \text{ or } [Wh/m^2K]$$

The heat conductivity of a material is determined by the *coefficient of thermal conductivity* λ [W/mK]. It specifies the transition of heat – given in W/m^2 – through a 1-m-thick wall at a temperature difference of one degree.

The speed at which a building material absorbs or releases heat is called the heat penetration coefficient b that is determined by the specific heat capacity, the apparent density and the thermal conductivity:

$$b = \sqrt{c \cdot \rho \cdot \lambda} \ [kJ/ K \ m^2 \ h^{0.5}]$$

The larger the b-value of a material is, the faster heat will penetrate it, and it will appear cooler to the touch since the heat of the hand is transmitted faster.

Thermal bridges

Thermal bridges (sometimes erroneously called "cold bridges") denote patches on walls or roofs that have a significantly lower thermal resistance than adjacent areas. This means that at these patches, heat transition from the inside out is substantially higher than at areas with high thermal resistance. Consequently, they increase heat losses of the building and can even cause moisture problems due to the formation of condensate. This can lead to serious problems in the areas in question if there is no sufficient vapour proofing: moisture-affected areas will provide even poorer thermal insulation and, in the case of straw, may assist growth of moulds, spores, and bacteria. Risk areas for thermal bridges at straw bale walls are – for instance – unfilled gaps between bales or junctions with door and window frames. But even the wooden post-and-beam structure can form a thermal bridge since the thermal conductivity of wood is three to five times higher than that of straw bales.

Thermal insulation

One major advantage of the use of straw bales in building construction is that they provide excellent thermal insulation. This mainly depends on the density of the bales, the position of the stalks (parallel or perpendicular to the direction of heat transition) and the humidity content of the straw; to a lesser degree also the type of straw has to be taken into account.

The influence of humidity on thermal conductivity is, however, much lower than is the case with mineral building materials. According to Bauer (2000), the thermal conductivity is increased only by 1 to 7% while the same increase of humidity would enhance thermal conductivity in a brick wall to a much higher degree: according to Cammerer, a brick wall with a moisture content of 8% has a heat conductivity coefficient of $\lambda = 0.6$ W/mK; at 18% this value

is 0.8 W/mK.

Test results for the determination of the heat conductivity coefficient of straw vary a great deal. Depending on testing conditions, density, the position of the stalks and humidity content, the values range from 0.0337 to 0.086 W/mK (McCabe 1993). Various tests in Germany and Austria confirmed a value of $\lambda_{10,tr} = 0.045$ W/mK (**for vertical dry straw bales** at an average temperature of 10 °C), which is conform with EU standards. An assumed λ-value of 0.045 W/mK (**for vertical straw fibres**) amounts to a heat transmission coefficient – or U-value – of 0.12 W/m²K (R-value = 8.3) for a straw bale wall with a total thickness of 42 cm, a 35-cm straw layer and a total plaster thickness of 7 cm including plaster base. For a timber post-and-beam structure this amounts to a value of approx. 0.14 W/m²K (R-value = 7.1) for the entire wall; this value complies with the passive house standard of ≤ 0.15 W/m²K (R-value = 6.7) (Feist, 1996). The exact calculation of λ for the respective wall types with horizontal or vertical straw bales is stated in table 6.1. An assumed heat conductivity of 0.06 W/mK (**for horizontal straw fibres**) amounts to a U-value of 0.12 W/m²K (R-value = 8.3) for the entire wall. However, the overall wall thickness of horizontally installed bales is larger than that of vertical straw bales if similar thermal insulation is to be achieved. In our example, the bales would then have a thickness of 50 cm plus 7 cm of plaster.

6.1 U-value calculation

Determination of U-value, A	Thickness d(m)	λ (W/mk)	d/λ (m²K/W)
Thermal transmission, inside			0.130
Earth plaster/plaster base	0.025	0.80	0.031
Lathing	0,020	0.13	0.150
Vertical straw bales	0.350	0.045	7.777
Lathing	0.020	0.13	0.150
Lime plaster/plaster base	0.025	0.87	0.020
Thermal transmission, outside			0.040

Total U-value: U = 1/8.298 =   **0.12 W/m²K (R-value = 8.3)**
Total U-value incl. timber structure (8 %)   **U = 0.14 W/m²K (R-value = 7.1)**

Determination of U-value, B	Thickness d(m)	λ (W/mk)	d/λ (m²K/W)
Thermal transmission, inside			0.130
Earth plaster/plaster base	0.025	0.80	0.031
Lathing	0.020	0.13	0.150
Horizontal straw bales	0.500	0.060	8.333
Lathing	0.020	0.13	0.150
Lime plaster/plaster base	0.025	0.87	0.020
Thermal transmission, outside			0.040

Total U-value: U = 1/8.8543 =   **0.11 W/m²K (R-value = 9.1)**
Total U-value incl. timber structure (6 %)   **U = 0.12 W/m²K (R-value = 8.3)**

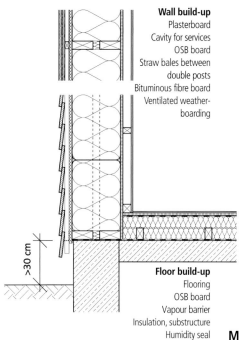

Wall build-up
Plasterboard
Cavity for services
OSB board
Straw bales between
double posts
Bituminous fibre board
Ventilated weather-
boarding

Floor build-up
Flooring
OSB board
Vapour barrier
Insulation, substructure
Humidity seal
Slab

>30 cm

left 6.2 Bales above splash water zone (Vertical and horizontal section)
right 6.3 Splash water zone with protected bales (Vertical and horizontal section)

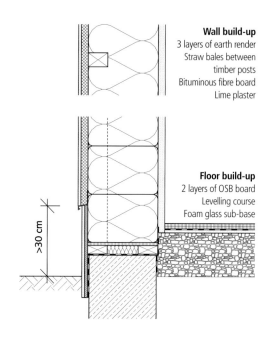

Wall build-up
3 layers of earth render
Straw bales between
timber posts
Bituminous fibre board
Lime plaster

Floor build-up
2 layers of OSB board
Levelling course
Foam glass sub-base

>30 cm

Moisture protection

Exterior walls have to be protected against humidity/water from all sides. The following passages will describe various methods to achieve this.

Horizontal seals against rising humidity

Building regulations in Germany stipulate that walls must be protected from rising humidity from the building ground by horizontal seals – regardless of whether it is a solid or lightweight construction.

Splash water protection

All walls must have a splash boarding at the base up to a height of at least 30 cm. Ideally, the first layer of straw bales should start above this height (*6.2*) or a splash protection consisting of splash boarding or special plaster has to be provided (*6.3*). The risk of splash water can be reduced significantly by a gravel or crushed stone bed or a dense and low vegetation at the perimeter (*6.5*). Hard floors in front of the wall will have the reverse effect (*6.4*).

Weather protection

Like any other wall, a straw bale wall needs to be protected from rain, hail and wind. This can be achieved with a weather-proof plaster free of cracks or – more preferably – by ventilated weather boarding (refer to chapter eight).

Protection against the formation of condensate as a result of vapour diffusion

Due to the vapour pressure gradient – which, in heated rooms in our climate, runs from the interior to the exterior – the water vapour in the air will find a way through the separating building element. This process follows the physical laws of pressure balance and is called diffusion.

The resistance of a material to the diffusion of water vapour in the air is called *vapour diffusion coefficient μ*. This μ-value depends on the density and pore structure of the respective material.

The product of vapour diffusion coefficient m and the thickness s of the building element equals the resistance to water vapour diffusion and is given as the diffusion-equivalent air layer thickness s_d [m]. Air has a vapour diffusion coefficient of 1; this means, for example, that a building element with $s_d = 10$ m has the same resistance to water vapour diffusion as a 10-m-thick air layer. As a rule of thumb, resistance to water vapour diffusion of the individual layers of a wall should decrease from the inside out. In some straw bale walls the reverse can be the case: if the wall is rendered with earth on the inside and with cement on the outside, vapour diffusion will be obstructed by the more vapour-resistant cement plaster; this may assist formation of condensate on the inside of the cement render. This is down to the low μ-value of earth render of 6 to 8 (refer to 6.6) and – in contrast – the high μ-value of cement render of 20 to 30. Even if the interior render were two to three times thicker than the exterior render, the resistance to water vapour diffusion of the exterior render would still remain substantially higher. The problem could be solved with an exterior lime render with a μ-value of 10. Alternatively, the vapour diffusion resistance of the interior earth render would have to be increased by a moisture-proof, vapour-resistant coat of paint.

The μ-value of straw bales is approximately 2.5 (GrAT 2001, page 38)

According to physical calculations in regard to vapour resistance, the indoor s_d-value should be ten times the s_d-value of the exterior layer beyond the insulation. At the same time, s_d should not exceed 5 m so at least a part of the humidity inside the bales can diffuse to the interior of the building.

$$s_{d\ interior} \geq 10 \cdot s_{d\ exterior}$$
$$s_{d\ interior} \leq 5 \text{ m}$$

In winter, it would be theoretically possible that the humidity content inside a straw bale wall increases as a result of condensation – compromising the thermal insulation. However, long-term tests on houses ren-

dered on both sides conducted by Canada Mortgage and Housing Corporation found that the humidity content of the bales was relatively constant at an average of 13.4 % (Steen et al, 1994; Jolly 2000).

Further research by Stroh Tec GmbH, Austria found that local condensation within a building element – as is typically caused by locally restricted thermal bridges – remains limited for a relatively long period and does not expand due to capillary action as in earth. Additionally, if the wall structure is open to vapour diffusion, moisture can escape relatively fast (Pfleiderer, page 36). Generally, the moisture content of the straw bales should not exceed 15 %. If this value is exceeded for a limited period this will not result in decay; however, it will reduce thermal insulation.

In spaces with a humidity of more than 70 % – for example bathrooms – it is advisable to increase the resistance to water vapour diffusion of the interior render, for example by additives like linseed-oil varnish or resistant coats of paint like latex or linseed-oil varnish (also refer to chapter eight). A vapour barrier course is usually not required for a vapour-permeable wall with exterior lime plaster or ventilated weather boarding.

With regard to the early straw bale buildings in the USA, which were plastered with cement and had no vapour barrier, it should be mentioned that there are no reports on damages as a result of condensate. It can be assumed with certainty that condensate will form inside the wall, but in such small quantities that it does not pose any danger.

from top to bottom
6.4 Splashing on hard surfaces
6.5 Reduction of splashing

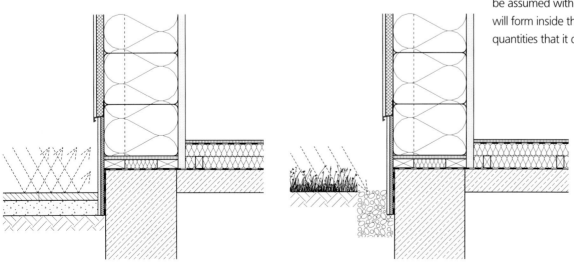

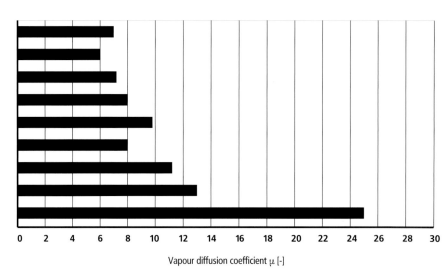

Earth, high clay (C) content (C = 28 %, Si = 34 %, Sa = 38 %)	
Earth, high silt (Si) content (C = 12 %, Si = 78 %, Sa = 14 %)	
Earth, high sand (Sa) content (C = 15 %, Si = 29 %, Sa = 56 %)	
Earth render, high clay content	
Earth render, high silt content	
Trass-lime (eminently hydraulic lime) render	
Lime render	
Lime-casein render (10/1)	
Lime-cement render	

Vapour diffusion coefficient μ [-]

above 6.6 μ-values of earth renders (Minke 2000)
below 6.7 Sorption curves of rye and wheat straw (GrAT 2001 and Minke 2000)

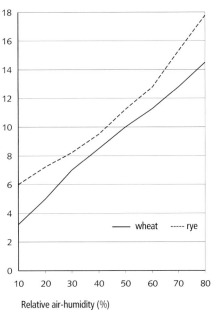

Water content (%)

Relative air-humidity (%)

— wheat ----- rye

Equilibrium moisture

According to the laws of diffusion, a humid building element surrounded by unsaturated air should gradually dry out completely. However, this is only partially the case: building materials may contain small air enclosures or porous material may contain capillary moisture. Therefore, every *dry* building material contains a specific rest of moisture – also called *equilibrium moisture*. This depends on the temperature and surrounding relative air-humidity. The higher the air-humidity is, the more humidity the material will extract of the surrounding air and its equilibrium moisture will rise: this process is called *sorption* or *absorption*. Conversely, for the emission of humidity by the material the term *desorption* is used. *Sorption* is also used as the generic term for both processes. Sorption is based on the ability of a material to store entering water molecules at the walls of pores. Consequently, the equilibrium moisture represents the maximum amount of moisture that a material will absorb at any given temperature and constant air-humidity; it is also called *hygroscopic* moisture. The percentage of water contained in a material is usually given as the mass-specific water content U_m. It is calculated as follows:

$$U_m = \frac{\text{mass of the stored water}}{\text{mass of dry building material}}$$

The dependence of the sorption of building materials on the relative air-humidity is represented in so-called *sorption curves* or *sorption isotherms* – the term isotherm meaning that the absorbed air-humidity-specific amount of water is measured at constant respective temperatures. Figure *6.7* shows the sorption curves of wheat straw at 25 °C and of rye straw at 21 °C.

Methods for the measurement of moisture content

Due to the inhomogeneous structure of straw, it is difficult to determine its moisture content. An exact determination is possible by comparing the specific weight of the bales before and after drying. It can also be tested by measuring electric conductivity: two brass electrodes will be placed into the bale at a determined distance and the electric current is measured; various factors will influence the results: the position of the straw stalks (parallel or perpendicular to the electrodes), the existence of cavities, load and temperature.

According to Götte (1966), a temperature difference of 1 °C will cause a deviation of the result by about 0.1 % and the changing of the superimposed load by 10 N (= 1 kg) will cause a deviation of 2.5 %.

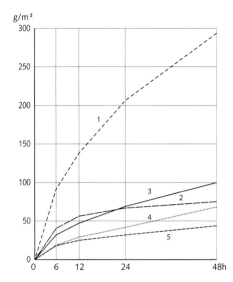

1 Earth, high clay content   4 Lime-cement render
2 Earth render   5 Stucco
3 Planed spruce

right 6.8 Sorption curves of renders at 21 °C and at an increase of space air-humidity from 50 % to 80 %; sample thickness: 15 mm (Minke 2000)

A simpler method for the establishment of the quantitative moisture content is called *hygrometric method* and is based on the principle of equilibrium moisture: here, a probe is introduced into the bale and the relative air-humidity in the bale is measured. With the assistance of the sorption isotherm the percentage of humidity inside the bale can then be derived from the correlation of the relative exterior air-humidity and the air-humidity within the bale (refer to figure 6.7).

Moisture balance

Clay – more than any other solid building material – has very positive effects on the balance of air-humidity in an indoor space due to its excellent sorption properties. If, for example, air-humidity in a room rises above 50 %, clay will absorb moisture and – in reverse – if it drops below 50 % earth will release it. This process is called sorption. Figure 6.8 shows the sorption curves of various kinds of plaster at a temperature of 21 °C and at an increase of indoor air-humidity from 50 % to 80 %; Figure 6.9 shows the respective values for an increase from 30 % to 70 %. It follows that earth render has the highest and stucco the lowest sorption capability and that fibrous additives facilitate sorption. Figure 6.10 shows the sorption and desorption curves of customary ready-mixed earth renders: it is evident that sorption can vary a lot between different products and depends on the kind and content of clay as well as on organic addi-

tives. The good sorption performance of loose straw bears no practical significance for the indoor humidity balance, as the bales used for building straw bale walls are highly compressed and rendered, slowing down the sorption process considerably. Therefore, it is advisable to apply a relatively thick, multi-layered earth render to straw bale walls. Even better sorption is provided by interior walls built of "green" unfired bricks whose sorptive capacity is distinctly stronger due to their high clay content (also see curve 1, "earth, high clay content", in figures 6.8 and 6.9). For further information on the humidity-regulating effect of earth, see Minke, 2000, chapter 1.4.4.

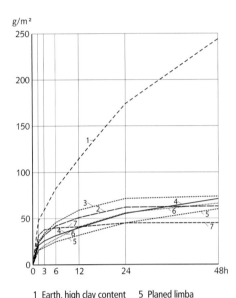

1 Earth, high clay content   5 Planed limba
2 Earth render   (African timber)
3 Earth render with coco   6 Lime-cement render
   fibres   7 Stucco
4 Planed spruce

above 6.9 Sorption curves of renders at 21 °C and at an increase of space air-humidity from 30 % to 70 %; sample thickness: 15 mm (Minke 2000)

right 6.10 Sorption and desorption curves of various ready-mixed earth-renders (Minke 2003)

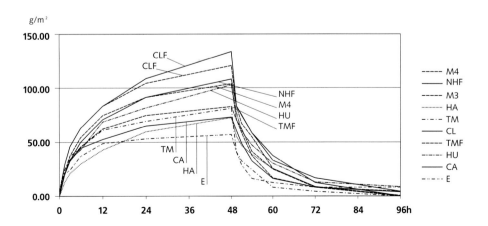

Wind and air tightness

Modern and highly insulated buildings like *Low Energy* and *Passive Houses* require a high grade of air-tightness; otherwise, the performance of thermal insulation will be considerably reduced. Furthermore, gaps and fissures to the interior finishes of external walls may assist the risk of condensation (refer to chapter six).

While fissure-free renders can easily provide air-tightness for load-bearing straw bale walls, framed timber structures with exposed woodwork may assist the formation of gaps between timber members and render. It has to be made sure that all gaps, between the actual bales and between bales and primary structure, are carefully sealed: this can be achieved by tight packing of the bales and supplementary stuffing of remaining cavities. Weak points are window frames, areas below ring beams or ceiling panels, respectively; these also have to be sealed carefully.

Fire protection

Building materials are classified with regard to their fire resistance as follows: F30, F60, F90, F120. In steps of 30 minutes, these classifications highlight the capability of the respective materials to maintain their essential functions such as structural integrity and the enclosure of space.

Authorised research in Austria established that bales of untreated wheat straw with an apparent density of 120 kg/m³ possess a normal inflammability. By contrast, a non-loadbearing straw bale wall with interior earth render and exterior lime render was assigned an F90 fire rating. Various tests in Germany and Austria confirmed these results, and related tests in the USA (SHB AGRA test) even established fire resistance of 120 minutes (Steen et al. 1994).

The high fire resistance of a plastered straw bale wall can be attributed to the high fire rating of the render itself as well as the high compression of the bales not leaving enough oxygen for the combustion of

right 6.11 Fire test at the Research Laboratory for Experimental Building, University of Kassel, 2000

straw. Even if the plaster contains cracks, a charred exterior straw layer will be formed preventing the entrance of further oxygen. This result was established under high temperature conditions of 1,000 °C. The test installation of the Research Laboratory for Experimental Building at the University of Kassel is pictured on image *6.11*: the plaster cracked, as it had not dried out completely and the fire was applied punctually. Unfinished, exposed straw bale walls may pose an increased fire hazard due to protruding straw stubbles. Therefore, they

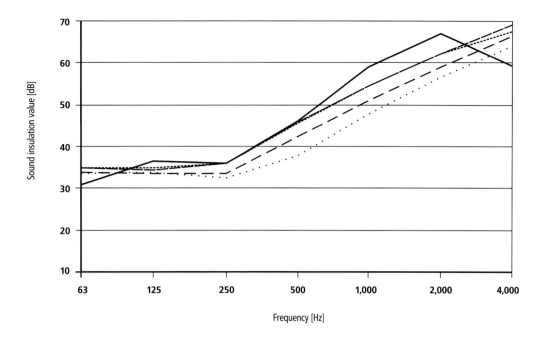

6.14

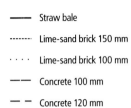

—— Straw bale

······· Lime-sand brick 150 mm

· · · · Lime-sand brick 100 mm

— — Concrete 100 mm

— — Concrete 120 mm

should receive a first plaster layer right after completion of the wall structure. For best results, a pump should be used to spray and immerse all stalks evenly (refer to images *6.12* and *6.13*).

130 kg/m³ and untreated 2.5 to 3.5 cm earth render as established at Technical University Eindhoven, the Netherlands. Here, they are compared to solid concrete and sand-lime masonry walls.

Sound insulation

Air-borne sound insulation mainly depends on the weight (mass) of a building element: the greater the weight of a wall, the better is the air-borne sound insulation it will provide. Sound insulation of straw bales with double-sided plastering is higher than that of single-layered elements of the same weight. This fact can be attributed to a certain vibration of straw bales, and bales will also absorb sound to a certain degree. In Australia, tests were conducted on 45-cm-thick walls of a sound studio: at a noise level of 114 to 117 dB inside the building, 62 to 71 dB were measured outside within a frequency spectrum of 500 to 10,000 Hz. This amounts to a noise level difference of 43 to 55 dB (John Glassford in GrAT 2001).

Figure *6.14* shows the sound insulation measures of a 45-cm-thick straw bale wall with an apparent density of 120 to

7 Designing a straw bale building

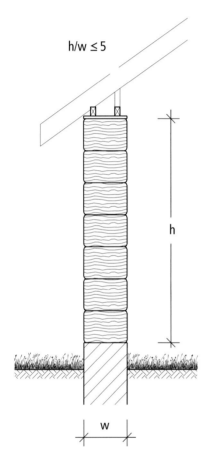

h/w ≤ 5

h

w

Special aspects of load-bearing straw bale walls

As straw bales will be compressed by an imposed load, the following precautions have to be taken for load-bearing straw bale walls:

– The roof load has to be distributed evenly to all walls. Loads must not be concentrated on any spot.
– Roof loads have to be transmitted centrically and have to be distributed over at least 50 % of the wall thickness.
– The ratio of wall height to wall thickness should not exceed 5:1 (7.1).
– Straw bales have to be highly compressed and possess a density of at least 90 kg/m³.
– Window openings should be rather narrow – but in any event higher than wide (7.2).
– As far as possible, lintels above windows and doors should be avoided. Instead,

the ring beam should be appropriately dimensioned to accommodate this task.
– In case lintels are intended, sufficient tolerance to the ring beam has to be allowed for, as the straw bales tend to creep during the first weeks or months after completion.
– Dimensions between wall openings as well as openings to corners have to equal at least one bale length (7.2).
– For particularly long and slender walls and in the event of very high roof loads, provisions for additional bracing have to be made to avoid buckling.

Images 7.3 to 7.6 show options for interesting roof structures ensuring a largely even distribution of forces onto the walls. Other suitable forms are pyramidal roofs, whereas common pitched or hipped roofs can cause structural problems. These roof types can only be applied if they are extremely lightweight or if the walls are highly prestressed.

above 7.1 Required wall proportion: w/h ≤ 1/5
right 7.2 Design of wall openings

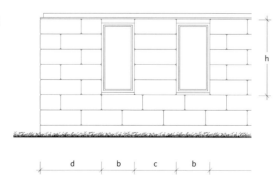

h

d   b   c   b

7.3 to 7.6 Octagonal and square Hogan roofs (Design: Minke 1983)

Special aspects of non-loadbearing straw bale walls

In case of the erection of framed structures with straw infill panels, the position of posts in relation to the bales has to be considered already at design stage. Image 7.7 features the four different configurations possible. If posts are positioned on the interior or exterior of the straw bale layer (positions A and C), the bale length has to be considered only for window and door openings. If the posts are positioned between bales (B and B') the structural grid should be conveniently based on the bale length; this would entail equal window and door widths, respectively.

The use of latticed posts (B') can be advantageous, as no additional substructure for exterior weatherboarding will be required. Furthermore, the bales fit snugly between the posts, thus providing a relatively firm work base.

If bales of different lengths are used and if the structural grid follows primarily structural considerations without regard to bale dimensions, posts should preferably be positioned inside or outside of the straw bale wall: in either case, bales should be laid in a "running bond", avoiding continuous vertical joints (refer to 7.2 and 7.9).

If posts are positioned in cut-out gaps as shown in figure 7.7, solution D, this can create a better base for interior lining, reduce the overall wall thickness and facilitate the fixing of furniture. Image 7.8 pictures such a gap that was cut out with a chain saw. The following paragraphs will deal with respective structural details of individual wall elements and present detailed drawings of advisable solutions.

above 7.8 Cut-out gaps for posts
right 7.7 Possible positions of posts

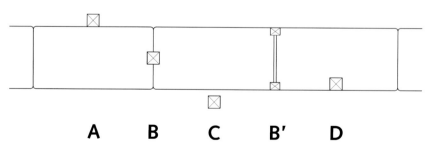

A B C B' D

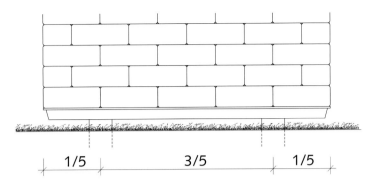

| 1/5 | 3/5 | 1/5 |

Detailing of foundations

The type of foundation of a building will – above all – depend on the frost line and load-bearing capabilities of the ground. In the particular case of straw bale walls, their relatively great thickness entails larger – and therefore more expensive – foundations. One solution to bypass this problem may be the provision of a beam supported by point foundations, also known as periodic reinforced piers or elephant's feet, as shown in figure 7.9.

As the test building discussed in chapter ten shows, this is also an economical solution. Another financially viable method may be the construction of strip foundations out of locally resourced natural stone or recycled bricks – provided the owners build them on their own account.

Yet another cost-effective solution may be the construction of a floating floor slab on an insulation layer of crushed foam glass (refer to figure 7.10). The crushed glass layer consists of foamed recycled glass in a size range of 0 to 90 mm. The layer is compacted with a vibrator, and in a highly compacted state it has a heat conductivity of 0.08 W/mK whereas in a loose state the λ-value is 0.06 W/mK. This build-up also does without a waterproofing course since the closed cells of the foamed glass intercept capillary action.

A rather unconventional but very economical do-it-yourself solution is the use of disposed car tyres filled with lean concrete: the tyres can be resourced free of charge from petrol stations or car tyre dealers, and the amount of required concrete will be low if demolition rubbish and rocks are used as aggregate.

above 7.9 Structurally optimised positioning of point foundations
right 7.10 Crushed foam glass layer acting as insulation and water-proofing course
below 7.11 Base detail

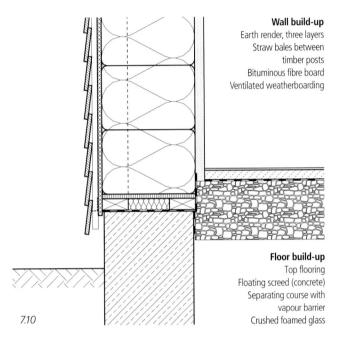

Wall build-up
Earth render, three layers
Straw bales between timber posts
Bituminous fibre board
Ventilated weatherboarding

Floor build-up
Top flooring
Floating screed (concrete)
Separating course with vapour barrier
Crushed foamed glass

7.10

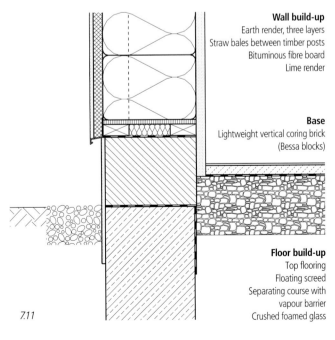

Wall build-up
Earth render, three layers
Straw bales between timber posts
Bituminous fibre board
Lime render

Base
Lightweight vertical coring brick
(Bessa blocks)

Floor build-up
Top flooring
Floating screed
Separating course with vapour barrier
Crushed foamed glass

7.11

from top to bottom
*7.12 Base consisting
of pallets
7.13 Base consisting
of recycled car tyres
7.14 Base detail with
rebate to suit flush
render and gravel
course*

Base details

Besides providing a splash skirting for the straw bale wall, a base or plinth has to fulfil numerous tasks: it has to be waterproof, pressure-proof and intercept capillary action, and must also provide sufficient thermal insulation.

These requirements can be met with lightweight Bessa blocks with an exterior layer of waterproof render (*7.11*). However, as this render acts as a vapour barrier the base should receive an interior vapour-proof finish as well.

In the event that interior spaces are flooded, water may soak the straw bales: thus, it is advisable to start the first layer of straw bales a few centimetres above the finished floor level (*7.11*).

Figures *7.12* and *7.13* show experimental do-it-yourself solutions using used tyres and pallets. It has to be made sure that voids and cavities of the pallets are filled with insulating material like polystyrene pellets and that they are coated with waterproof material like bubble wrap. The car tyres can be filled with lean concrete.

Figure *7.14* shows a solution from Australia by Frank Thomas: here, a rebate in the floor slab accommodates the exterior render to prevent cracking as a result of sagging of the render. Floor planks lift the bales slightly and facilitate the threading of tensioning wires for prestressing of the walls.

A crushed stone or gravel bed under the bales traps condensate that might otherwise assist decay of the bales. The bales should not directly touch a foil or a bituminous fibre board. For more base details, see page 42.

Wall build-up

Position of the posts

Since the cutting or customising of straw bales is a strenuous procedure (refer to chapter nine), the structural grid and the position and size of wall openings should coincide with the bale dimensions. Furthermore, the position of the posts inside or in front of or behind the bales, as well as the decision as to whether to use simple or composite posts – for instance double T or latticed posts – is of crucial importance for site procedures, detailing and interior fit-out (refer to figures *7.15* to *7.17*).

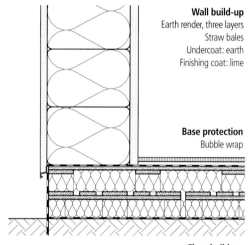

Wall build-up
Earth render, three layers
Straw bales
Undercoat: earth
Finishing coat: lime

Base protection
Bubble wrap

Floor build-up
OSB board
Vapour barrier
Two layers of pallets with insulation filling
Moisture barrier

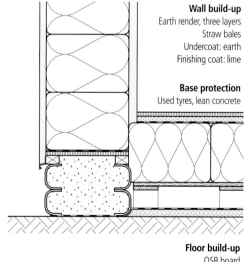

Wall build-up
Earth render, three layers
Straw bales
Undercoat: earth
Finishing coat: lime

Base protection
Used tyres, lean concrete

Floor build-up
OSB board
Levelling course
Vapour barrier
Straw bales
Pallets
Moisture barrier

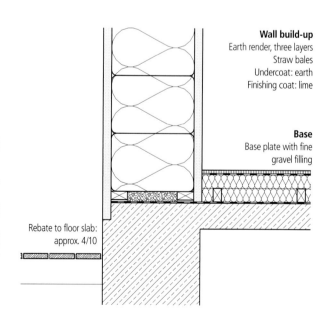

Wall build-up
Earth render, three layers
Straw bales
Undercoat: earth
Finishing coat: lime

Base
Base plate with fine
gravel filling

Rebate to floor slab:
approx. 4/10

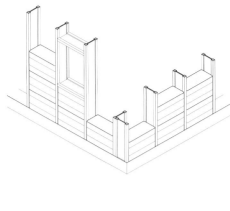

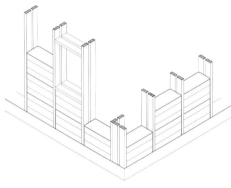

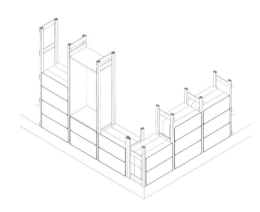

If the straw bales are positioned in front of or behind the primary structure, they must be fixed to it unless the bales are exceptionally prestressed between foundation and ring beam.

The position of posts in relation to the surface of the bales bears substantial consequences on the finishing and interior fit-out: if the posts sit flush with the interior face of the bales, an additional plaster base will be required (for example a matting of reed).

To prevent expansion or shrinkage cracks, the use of an additional plaster reinforcement mesh is advisable.

Positioning the posts in front of a straw bale wall that is to be plastered is time-consuming, and cracks between render and timber are unavoidable.

If the interior is to be lined with gypsum fibreboard, hard fibreboard, OSB, chipboard or plasterboard, the posts should be spaced so that they suit the board dimensions. This also applies to the fixing of an exterior venti-lated weatherboarding.

Bracing against horizontal forces

As straw bales do not contribute to the stiffening of a wall structure, the timber post-and-beam structure – like other conventional buildings – has to be braced against horizontal forces (wind loads). In this context, the construction of individual posts within the bales is a rather difficult solution as the cross-bracings between posts will obstruct

installation of the bales. Therefore, composite posts with a width equalling the thickness of the bales should be preferred: in this case, bracing is provided by diagonal boarding, sprockets or rigid panels like OSB boards (refer to figure 7.18).

Position of straw bales

Straw bales can be installed in horizontal or vertical position. When installed vertically, the stalks will stand vertical as well, thus providing better thermal insulation (the heat conductivity coefficient λ perpendicular to the fibres is lower than the one along the fibres) and reducing the wall thickness. On the other hand, for vertically installed bales, a plaster base will be required to render the surfaces.

Interconnection of the bales and connection of bales to the bearing structure

The building regulations of New Mexico, USA, stipulate precise rules for the construction of non-loadbearing straw bale walls: the straw bales should be placed between the timber posts and connected to them by expanded metal angles. The lowest two bale layers must be tied to the foundation via steel rods with at least two rods per one bale (refer to figure 7.19). Additionally, the upper bale layers must also be interconnected with steel rods. These provisions are very labour-intensive and might – under European climatic conditions – assist condensa-

from top to bottom
7.15 H-profile posts
7.16 Solid timber posts
7.17 latticed »ladder profile« posts

right 7.18 Bracing against horizontal forces
7.19 Bale connection detail according to New Mexico Code

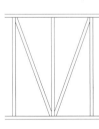

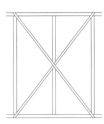

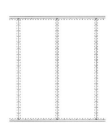

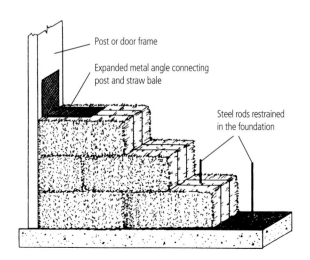

Post or door frame

Expanded metal angle connecting post and straw bale

Steel rods restrained in the foundation

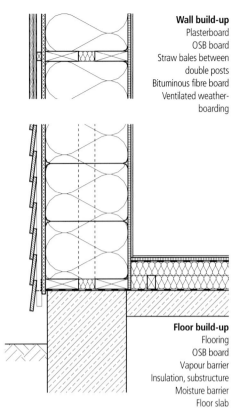

Wall build-up
Plasterboard
OSB board
Straw bales between
double posts
Bituminous fibre board
Ventilated weather-
boarding

Floor build-up
Flooring
OSB board
Vapour barrier
Insulation, substructure
Moisture barrier
Floor slab

tion on the steel rods and thus potentially result in damages to the building. After all, these rods are not required if bales are pre-stressed between foundation or grade beam and ring beam or inferior purlin as described in chapters nine and ten. The pre-stressing will create sufficient friction at the joints between bales and between bales and primary structure, usually making additional connections unnecessary.

Wall junctions with foundation, base and floor

The detailing of the lower junction of wall and foundation and floor must ensure that there are no thermal bridges and that the straw and earth render in that area is protected from splash water. Figures *7.20* to *7.22* show some possible solutions:

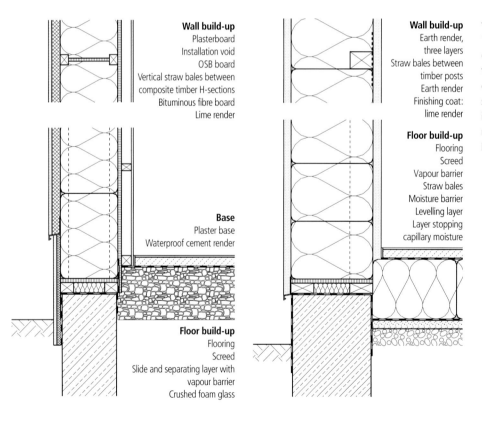

Wall build-up
Plasterboard
Installation void
OSB board
Vertical straw bales between
composite timber H-sections
Bituminous fibre board
Lime render

Base
Plaster base
Waterproof cement render

Floor build-up
Flooring
Screed
Slide and separating layer with
vapour barrier
Crushed foam glass

Wall build-up
Earth render,
three layers
Straw bales between
timber posts
Earth render
Finishing coat:
lime render

Floor build-up
Flooring
Screed
Vapour barrier
Straw bales
Moisture barrier
Levelling layer
Layer stopping
capillary moisture

from top to bottom
7.20 to 7.22 Junction details of foundation, floor and base complying with the structural and building-physical requirements (vertical and horizontal sections)

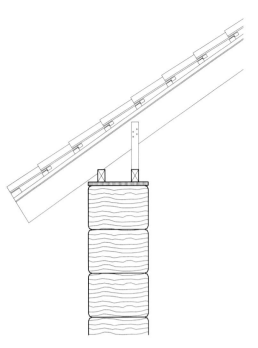

Ring beams

The ring beam – that is, the upper wall junction – will perform multiple tasks: it receives the roof loads and distributes them evenly over the entire wall length; it stabilises the top course of straw bales and, hence, prevents buckling of the entire wall. It reinforces bracing of the wall corners and can also function as a lintel to door and window openings, provided they are not too big. Therefore, the ring beam has to be particularly bending-resistant or rigid and as wide as possible. Composite, *ladder*-type ring beams were found to be a preferable and economical solution for the even distribution of roof loads (*7.23*). Other options for the distribution of loads are chipboards or OSB boards, which are fixed underneath the actual ring beams (*7.24*). Lightweight ring beams with a high load-bearing capacity can be assembled out of composite timber H-sections (*7.25*).

In any event, roof loads have to be transmitted in the centre of the ring beam and the wall. Figure *7.26* shows a solution that complies with this requirement even when steep roofs are concerned.

Usually, ring beams are made of wood. There are built examples made of steel and reinforced concrete: however, they are usually not suitable for the Northern and Central European climates as they require relatively complicated insulation details to avoid thermal bridges.

above 7.26 Central transmission of loads at a steep pitched roof

right from top to bottom
7.23 Ring beam as composite ladder-type element
7.24 Ring beam with bottom boards for load distribution
7.25 Boxed ring beam made of composite timber H-sections

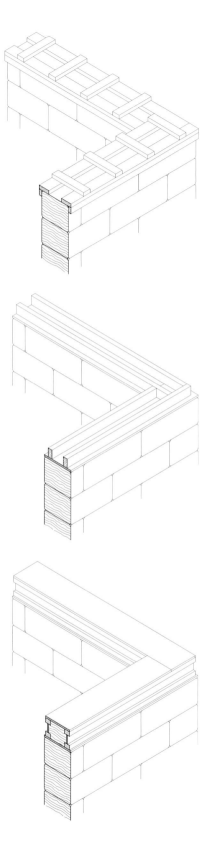

Windows and doors

Position and design of window and door junctions are of crucial importance to avoid damages to the building. The following discussion will concentrate on windows only since both windows and doors involve the same design issues.

If the window is recessed far back into the wall, a deep window sill built up high on both sides will be required to deal with snow and ice deposits. This position also carries the risk of a considerable thermal bridge at the window edge (7.30). A window that is positioned far outside also faces this problem. Furthermore, the space between the window jambs will not be ventilated properly, thus easily trapping condensation water that may assist the formation of moulds (7.31).

The mentioned problems can be mitigated by positioning the window into the middle of the opening – however, only an additional insulating pad will create a fully satisfactory solution (7.32).

The ideal solution in terms of the physical construction aspects is a casement window

(7.33): it excludes thermal bridges and provides better thermal insulation itself. Alternatively, a coupled window may be used (7.34). A weak spot externally is the joint between external plaster and window frame as water easily penetrates this joint. This problem can be solved by means of a cover profile with a sealing strip placed behind it or by integrating a sheet of damp-proof course underneath the render. Elastic joint fillers are less durable and are therefore not recommended at this point.

Corners can be reinforced to form a sharp edge (7.32) or slightly rounded (as shown in 7.33). Images 7.27 to 7.29 show a construction solution for curved windows used by Frank Thomas in Australia.

Figures 7.36 and 7.37 introduce solutions with timber or chipboard clad jambs instead of plastered embrasures.

This book does not cover other solutions that are typically used in timber construction: here, embrasures and wall finishes are usually clad with chipboard, plasterboard or gypsum fibreboard.

Rounded or chamfered (bevelled) corners as shown in figures 7.35 and 7.36 allow more light to enter the interior and create a more pleasant, gentle transition of light levels.

7.27 to 7.29

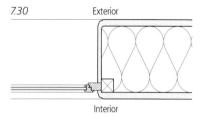

7.30 Exterior / Interior

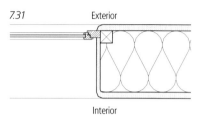

7.31 Exterior / Interior

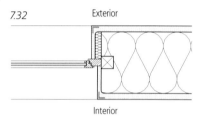

7.32 Exterior / Interior

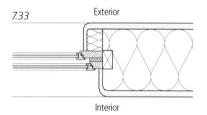

7.33 Exterior / Interior

7.30, 7.31
Unfavourable window position within the wall

7.32 Preferred window position with additional insulation to reduce thermal bridges
7.30 Ideal solution using casement

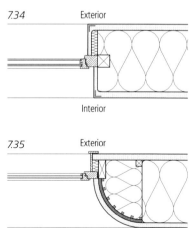

7.34 Exterior / Interior

7.35 Exterior / Interior

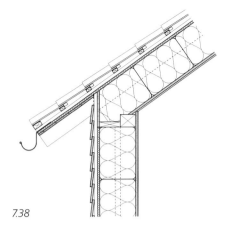

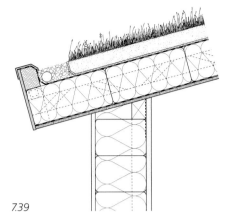

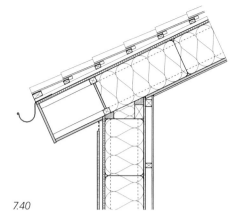

7.38   7.39   7.40

7.38 to 7.41 Possible
wall/roof junctions

Wall corners

Exterior corners generally form so-called
geometrical thermal bridges since at this
point the *cold* exterior wall area is proportionally larger than the *warm* interior wall
area. However, this effect will decrease as
the wall thickness increases; therefore, for
50-cm-strong straw bale walls this phenom-
enon can be neglected.
In the case of load-bearing straw bale walls,
the bales should interlock at the corners for
structural reasons; interlocking walls will
reinforce each other against horizontal
forces.

Wall/Roof junctions

Wall/roof junctions should prevent the formation of thermal bridges.
If the exterior surfaces are rendered, a sufficient roof overhang should be provided.
Ventilated exterior weatherboarding must
prevent snow or pelting rain from meeting
the exposed or earth-rendered surface of
the straw bales. Figures 7.38 to 7.41 show
various solutions for these tasks.
The junction detail of roof rafters has to
ensure that loads are transmitted in the centre of the ring beam to avoid torsion.

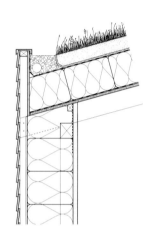

7.41

Interior walls

The construction of straw bale partitions
does not make much sense: unlike conventional partitions they require wide foundations and increase the cubical contents of
the building.
Furthermore, straw bale buildings provide
relatively little thermal mass and it is advisable to build interior walls from solid bricks,
possibly even natural stone. The most
favourable material for the indoor climate
are unfired earth bricks that have a high
heat storage capacity and – more than
other solid building materials – have the
capability to regulate air-humidity (refer
to chapter six).

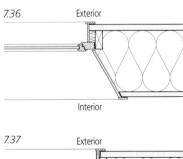

7.36   Exterior

              Interior

7.37   Exterior

              Interior

Intermediate ceilings

Intermediate ceilings in two-storey straw bale buildings are usually wooden joist or stacked plank ceilings. They have to ensure proper air-borne and footfall sound insulation. Image 7.42 shows a simple ceiling and floor build-up that is largely suitable for do-it-yourself construction: earth bricks positioned in-between the ceiling and floor layers improve air-borne sound insulation, provide thermal mass and balance air-humidity.

An entirely different but advantageous solution are vertically stacked planks (refer to image 7.43): here, a solid timber ceiling is formed by vertical closely stacked boards fixed together with nails or dowels. The advantage here is the low construction heigt and the good air-borne sound insulation without the need for additional structural measures. Furthermore, this ceiling type can be entirely or at least largely prefabricated, which allows fast installation – provided that a crane is used.

Service ducts

If possible, water pipes should not run inside straw bale walls; cold water pipes assist condensation leading to the soaking of the bales. In theory, this should not be a problem for hot water pipes, provided they are fully enclosed by the straw without any gaps or openings at joints or bents as is often the case in reality. A further disadvantage is the fact that leaks are hard to detect. Therefore, pipes should be integrated into the floor or stud walls, behind skirting boards (7.44) or they should be simply installed on top of the walls.

The same rules apply for electrical wires. If wires penetrate the straw layer, they have to be encased in a non-inflammable conduit or tubes. Sockets and switches are best integrated into door frames or on columns. If they need to be fixed where no timber backing is provided, it has to be ensured that they are firmly back-fixed to a batten

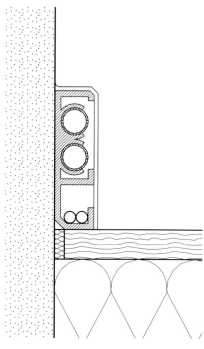

7.44

or wedge hammered into the straw bale or they could be fastened to a post with gypsum.

Heavy-duty fixings in straw bale walls

If the interior finish consists simply of plaster on the bales, an appropriate substructure has to be provided to enable the fixing of shelving, hanging cupboards, wall-mounted lights, heavy paintings and other fixtures. In most cases, this is not required if the interior is clad with timber, MDF or OSB boards. For the flexible fixing of pictures, a simple wooden batten (picture rail) may be provided on the top end of the wall.

Wall recesses

Straw bale walls provide the chance for creative sculptural wall design, as recesses for shelving, pictures or lights can be easily cut into the thick walls (refer to images 7.45, 7.46 and 7.48). Often a spot in the wall is intentionally exposed to reveal the wall's nature (7.47).

right 7.44 Skirting with integrated heating pipes and wiring duct

below 7.42 Wooden joist floor
7.43 Vertically stacked plank floor

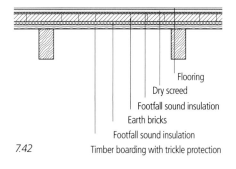

7.42

Flooring
Dry screed
Footfall sound insulation
Earth bricks
Footfall sound insulation
Timber boarding with trickle protection

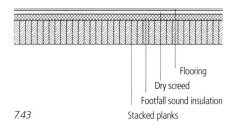

7.43

Flooring
Dry screed
Footfall sound insulation
Stacked planks

7.45

7.47

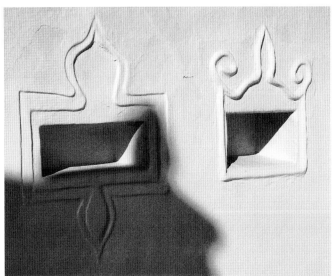

7.46

7.48

8 Surface protection and finishing works

8.1 Smoothing of the undercoat with a wooden board

Interior render

General rules

Rendering of straw bale surfaces is the simplest way of interior finishing. The render hardens and smoothes the bale surface and provides air-tightness and fire protection. Earth, stucco, lime, cement and lime-cement render are suitable products. Plasters should be reinforced at the corners and at joints of two different materials by a tension-proof mesh to prevent cracking.

Clay render

Due to its elasticity and its ability to balance air-humidity, earth render has a substantial advantage over all other render materials. As discussed earlier in chapter six – sorption and humidity regulation – earth render evidently absorbs more moisture at a given high air-humidity than other render materials and vice versa.

Usually, plaster is applied in three layers: the undercoat smoothes the bale surface and immerses sticking-out stalks. This layer should be applied with high pressure and is best sprayed on with a pump. The render should be rather liquid to penetrate a few centimetres beyond the surface. Stalk ends are smoothed over with a board or a trowel (8.1). The earth render should possess a high clay content to ensure strong adhesion to the straw stalks. The first layer will tend to creep and leave cracks as it dries: this is not hazardous, but rather increases adhesion of the top coats.

The second coat has to be leaner or, in other words, the contents of additives like sand and fine gravel need to be increased to reduce cracking during the drying process. Further suitable additives are saw dust or straw chaff or hemp fibres.

The main task of this coat is to roughly level the surface and prepare it for the top coat. Holes and uneven areas with a depth of more than 2 cm should be levelled with a mixture of chaff and earth before applying the second coat.

The finishing coat is 5 to 10 mm thick and forms the outer skin. Coarse sand, milled straw chaff, grain fibres or similar materials can be added to the earth to prevent cracking or improve the appearance. In this case, the contents of adhesive clay are to be reduced to 5 to 8 %. Therefore, it is important that the second coat is well moistened and, if needed, roughened up for better adhesion of the final coat. The plaster should be firmly thrown on and levelled. After initial drying, this final coat can be treated with a moist felt or sponge to create a rough finish of exposed coarse additives such as sand and straw.

The individual coats amount to an overall thickness of 3 to 6 cm. Generally speaking, the thermal insulation provided by the wall and the positive effects on air-humidity will be the better the thicker the overall plaster coat is.

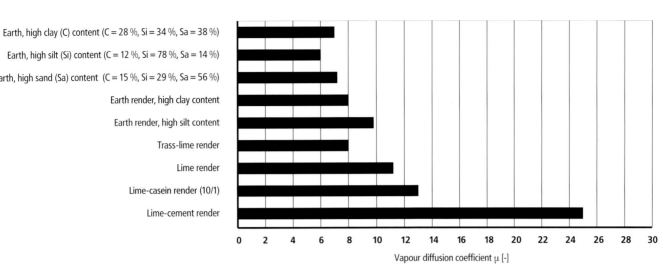

	Vapour diffusion coefficient μ [-]
Earth, high clay (C) content (C = 28 %, Si = 34 %, Sa = 38 %)	
Earth, high silt (Si) content (C = 12 %, Si = 78 %, Sa = 14 %)	
Earth, high sand (Sa) content (C = 15 %, Si = 29 %, Sa = 56 %)	
Earth render, high clay content	
Earth render, high silt content	
Trass-lime render	
Lime render	
Lime-casein render (10/1)	
Lime-cement render	

8.2 Vapour diffusion coefficient of various renders (Minke 2000)

Other kinds of render

To increase the strength or integrity of the plastered surface, the render coats can also be finished off with a lime top coat. In such an event, it is advisable to integrate a tension-proof reinforcement mesh. For further information on lime render, refer to this chapter, page 50.

Stucco is the material least favourable in terms of humidity balance and heat storage, and therefore it will not be discussed here in further detail.

Compared to earth render, cement plaster is fairly brittle and cracks will develop more easily as a result of movements of the substructure, wind loads or creeping of the bales. They should therefore be reinforced with glass fibre or metal meshes. Performance in terms of vapour diffusion and humidity balance is less favourable than that of earth render (refer to table *8.2*).

Exterior render

General rules

Exterior render materials have to prevent moisture form entering the straw bales and should, on the other hand, be vapour-permeable so that condensate can diffuse to the outside. Therefore, the vapour diffusion coefficient of the exterior plaster including a paint coat should be lower than that of the interior finish including a paint coat. Cement render has a relatively high resistance to vapour diffusion: a 40-mm-strong cement coat practically functions as a vapour barrier, as vapour diffusion only amounts to approx. 40 ng/Pa·s·m^2. By contrast, pure lime render has a vapour diffusion value of approx. 460 ng/Pa·s·m^2 while lime-cement render (1 part lime : 1 part cement : 6 parts sand) possesses a value of approx. 300 ng/Pa·s·m^2. An exterior latex paint coat would reduce that value to 200 ng/Pa·s·m^2 (values according to GrAT, 2002).

Earth render

Earth render is only suitable for exterior use if it is protected from rain or if additives or

8.3 Performance requirements of render on a loam base (Boenkendorf and Knöfel 1993)

Tested requirement	Performance
Plasticity/spread	17 ± 0.5 cm
Water resistance	> 90 %
Vapour diffusion coefficient μ	≤ 12
Adhesive strength $ß_{HZ}$	≥ 0.05 N/m^2
Compressive strength $ß_D$	3–5 N/mm^2
Flexural strength $ß_{BZ}$	1–1.5 N/mm^2
Tensile strength $ß_Z$	≥ 0.5 N/mm^2 according to the respective E modulus
Modulus of elasticity E_{dyn}	≤ 8,000 N/mm^2
Shrinkage ϵ_s	≤ 0.3 mm/m
Density	≤ 2.0 g/cm^2

8.4 Lime-casein render (according to Leszner and Stein 1987)

8.3 s_d-values of various paint products on earth render (Minke 2000)

paint coats increase its water resistance. Paint coats like linseed oil, varnish or latex, however, will substantially reduce vapour diffusion (refer to table *8.3*). They act as a vapour barrier and may lead to the collection of damaging condensation water within the bales, provided that the interior build-up does not include a vapour barrier or vapour-resistant paint coat.

A cement coat on top of an earth coat easily leads to damages: cement render is much less elastic than earth render, which may cause fissures under thermal or mechanical impact. If water penetrates those fissures, the earth will expand and chip off the top coat; this process may even be exacerbated by frost. In this context, lime render tends to cause far fewer problems, provided that cracks in the surface can be avoided.

Lime render

Lime render, which is sometimes also used in conjunction with cement as an additive, is a reliable exterior render material. It is of great importance that the bale surface is smoothed and all cavities and dents are filled beforehand with light clay mixed with straw. One should be aware of some details of the setting of lime render: it reacts with the carbon dioxide from the air to eventually form the compound $CaCO_3$. This process is very slow and takes place only in a moist environment; hence, at the first stage, the render must not dry out completely and needs to be protected from strong sunlight and – if required – needs to be watered. During the first weeks, it also has to be protected from pelting rain since at this stage it is easily washed off. Although setting is largely finished after three months, lime render reaches its final hardness only after three years.

It is advisable to add an extra 5 % of cement to speed up setting through hydraulic binding. The same goes for trass-lime (eminently hydraulic lime) render, which is also a hydraulic binder.

The undercoat should be applied with high pressure and is best sprayed on with a pump so that the stalks get fully immersed. The following two coats can be applied under use of a plaster base (matting of reed or metal mesh). The plaster base can be omitted but in any event a reinforcement mesh should be integrated into the second coat to prevent fissures. Micro-fissures of 0.2 mm or less can be painted over. Splash water protection is a crucial requirement and can be provided by means of water-

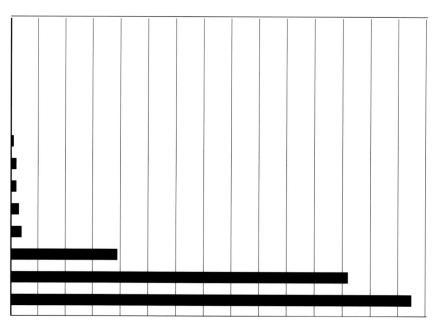

Finishing coats to earth render with high clay contents

Lime, 2 layers

Chalk-glue, 2 layers

Lime-casein (1/8)*, 2 layers

Lime-casein (1/1)*, 2 layers

Non-fat quark (German curd cheese), 1 layer

Sodium-water solution, 1 layer

Lime-casein linseed oil, 2 layers

Water-based silica paint, 2 layers

Emulsion paint, 2 layers

Beeswax paint, 2 layers

Latex paint, 2 layers

Linseed oil varnish, 1 layer

*Denotes mixture ratio.

Diffusion-equivalent air-layer thickness s_d [m]

repellent additives or paint coats, or a splash skirting.

Lime render is made up of 1 part lime and 3 to 4 parts sand. The lime can be used in the form of slaked lime (calcium hydroxide) or – as builders often recommend – stored wet-slaked lime that is produced by soaking lime pieces for months or years. This process is basically the storing of a soggy mass of slaked lime; over time, the heavier, coarser components will form a deposit on the bottom producing extremely smooth stuff at the top. After setting, this lime putty possesses a high elasticity. Also commercially available slaked lime should better be soaked for a number of days before being

Lime powder	Trass lime	Coarse sand	Non-fat quark	Linseed oil varnish	Clay, rich	Cow dung	Resulting μ-value
1	–	3	–	–	–	–	11.2
–	1	3	–	–	–	–	10.8
1	–	6	0.5	–	–	–	6.2
1	–	15	0.5	–	3	–	9.7
1	–	3	–	0.05	–	–	15.2
1	–	3	0.25	0.05	–	–	28.5
1.5	–	10	–	–	2	6	8.0

8.5 μ-values of various lime render types (Minke 2000) [mixture ratio]

used as render. The coarser lime deposits on the bottom should be used only as mortar for brickwork.

Publications dealing with the restoration of timber-framed houses often recommend trass-lime render instead of pure lime render. This render consists of an undercoat of 1 part trass-lime and 3 parts sand and a finishing coat of 1 part trass-lime and 2.5 parts sand.

Trass-lime is highly hydraulic lime consisting of calcium hydrate and trass powder. Hydraulic means that the materials bind water apart from carbon dioxide. There are pros and cons to this kind of render: hydraulic render sets quickly, but is very brittle and does not accommodate to creeping and movements of the wall as does the elastic lime render. For this reason, some builders have ceased to use trass-lime for

new buildings altogether, others recommend a mixture of 1 part trass-lime and 2 parts lime.

Analyses of historic buildings with lime render that often had remained intact for several hundred years found that the render did not exclusively consist of stored slaked lime putty but that, for instance, impurities and additional clay deposits had increased its strength. This is due to the fact that the acidic components of clay-like silicic acid, aluminium oxide, ferrous oxide etc. are hydraulic binding agents increasing strength and durability of the lime render (Wisser and Knöfel 1988). In historic lime render, hydraulic additives like pozzuolana (a natural volcanic lime-clay mixture from Pozzuoli near Naples) and trass, ash and brick-dust of historic bricks can also be found. Brick-dust of contemporary bricks, however, does not possess hydraulic properties since nowadays the bricks are fired under extremely high temperatures that destroy all potentially hydraulic agents like silicic, ferrous and aluminium compounds. Bricks that were fired at low temperatures maintain their hydraulic properties. In India, for instance, the so-called surkhi render consisting of 1 part lime and 2 to 4 parts brick-dust is still very common.

Historic lime render recipes are mostly based on higher sand and gravel contents and different grain sizes than are common nowadays. To be sure, the renders of former times contained additives like animal hair or bristle and casein. Casein – in earlier days also whey, non-fat milk or buttermilk were used – chemically reacts with lime to form the non-water soluble compound calcium albuminate.

Nowadays dairy products like cream cheese or soft curd with a maximum 1.5 % in fat can be used. Non-fat quark (German curd cheese) contains about 11 % casein. Casein reduces water absorption of the render – which is good in terms of weather protection – but unfortunately also slightly reduces vapour diffusion.

The Research Laboratory for Experimental Building at Kassel University successfully tested lime-casein render with a high casein content (non-fat quark : lime : sand, grain size 0–2 mm = 1 : 10 : 40) as a weather-resistant exterior plaster. Initially, the quark and lime have to be mixed to a thick paste without the use of water; reduced vapour diffusion has to be noted here (refer to table 8.5).

Another mixture (non-fat quark : lime : sand, grain size 0–1 mm = 1 : 6 : 25) is a favoured material for repairs of fissures and as a thin painted-on render coat.

In warmer climates, common salt is often added to lime render, as salt binds water and assists setting. Because of its high salt content, herring brine was used in the old days in Germany. This brine also contains stabilising proteins.

Table 8.3 shows how additives such as linseed oil varnish and non-fat quark reduce the vapour diffusion values of lime renders.

Application of lime top coats on earth undercoat

When a lime top coat is applied to an earth undercoat, as is commonly the case with exterior walls, sufficient adhesion between both layers has to be ensured. To achieve this, a coat of acetate of alumina could be applied to the earth undercoat. The first lime coat should have a grain size range up to 6 mm and has to be rubbed hard into the earth coat. Alternatively, the earth undercoat can also be keyed to achieve good bonding.

Cement render

Although from a contemporary point of view cement plaster is not suitable as an exterior render since it is very brittle and has a high vapour diffusion coefficient (also refer to the earlier paragraph *General rules*), it has to be mentioned that cement plaster was regularly used on the early straw bale buildings in Nebraska. The plaster was normally applied to a base of chicken wire, which was stitched together as shown in figure 8.6. This method succeeds without

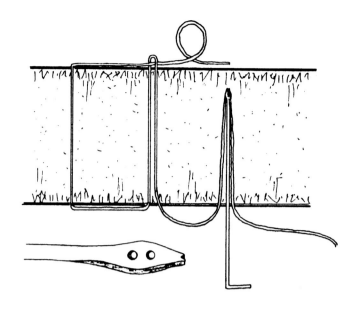

the otherwise required first sprayed-on plaster coat to immerse the straw stalks; on the other hand, this method creates undesirable gaps between the bales and the plaster coat that prevent moisture transport from the inside out. Builders in the USA, Canada and Australia continue to use this historically tried and tested building method. In Central Europe, it is not advisable due to the prevailing climate and physical reasons (refer to chapter six).

Paint coats

Exposed paint coats are deteriorated by mechanical forces like wind and frost and by chemical forces like ultraviolet radiation and acidic rain and have to be regularly renewed.

Exterior paint coats should be water-repellent and at the same time permeable to allow vapour diffusion. Moisture that penetrates the wall as a result of pelting rain or condensation has to be able to escape to the outside.

For this reason, latex, synthetic and emulsion (oil) paints are less suitable for this kind of use.

The diffusion-equivalent air-layer thickness (s_d) of various paint types is shown in table 8.3. s_d represents the thickness of an air-

8.6 Hand stitching of wire meshes acting as plaster base

layer equivalent to the thickness of a coat with the same vapour diffusion coefficient. The vapour diffusion coefficient equals the diffusion-equivalent air-layer thickness of a coat divided by the thickness of the coat or layer:

$$\mu = s_d/s$$

The following paragraphs discuss a number of tried and tested paints.

Pure lime whitewash

When preparing a whitewash, it has to be observed that the lime mix is fairly fluid; this will not cover up the render colour in one coat, however; rich covering and lime wash coats tend to chip off after drying. It is advisable to apply three to four thin coats. The mix should be made up of one 50-kg bag of calcium hydrate dissolved in 50 to 60 litres of water. Approximately 1 to 2 kg of common salt should be added to keep the paint coat moist as long as possible to speed up setting. In warmer climates, common salt is often added to lime render as salt binds water and assists setting. Because of its high salt content, herring brine was used in the old days. This brine also contains stabilising proteins and – as in lime-casein paint – assists the formation of non-water soluble calcium albuminate.

The first coat should be particularly thin so that the lime milk can penetrate the earth render finishing coat. Lime whitewash results in bright white surfaces. To tone the mixture down, fine clay powder or other earth colour pigments are suitable for use with lime. Under Middle European climatic conditions, an exterior lime whitewash will last approximately two to four years; pure lime whitewash is not wipe-resistant.

Lime-casein paint coat

Lime paint coats will get more durable and wipe-resistant when whey, non-fat quark or casein powder is added to the mixture. Non-fat quark contains about 11 % of casein. Lime and casein react chemically and form the compound calcium albuminate.

Historic lime whitewashes are often a mixture of slaked lime putty, non-fat milk or whey.

A tested and tried mixture ratio is 1 part non-fat quark, 1 to 3 parts lime and 1.5 to 2.5 parts of water. If linseed oil varnish is added at a maximum of 10 % of the quark contents, it will make the mixture more resistant to wiping but also more difficult to handle. The linseed oil has to be mixed in very carefully, ideally with a whisk, to create a smooth emulsion. To avoid segregation of the mixture and to maintain its consistency, the paint should be stirred occasionally and should be applied within two to four hours; the mixture can be tinted with pigments. (Note that linseed oil varnish reduces vapour diffusion.) In any event, lime-casein coats should be applied to dry surfaces only to prevent formation of moulds.

For wet rooms, the following mixture should be used: mix 1 part slaked lime putty with 5 parts non-fat quark for 1 to 2 minutes, add 20 parts of lime and mix in with 2 to 4 % linseed oil varnish and – finally – water down. For a wipe-resistant and water-repellent finish, two coats of paint are required; part of the lime can be replaced with pigments suitable for use with lime.

Borax-casein paint coats

Instead of lime, casein can also be mixed with Borax (a complex borate mineral) forming a non-water soluble compound comparable to the lime-casein mixture. If the Borax content is too high, it will crystallise and impair the visual appearance of the finish. Borax is colour-neutral and is therefore very suitable for paint mixtures with coloured additives. The mixture can be condensed and brightened with chalk. Adding clay powder will increase smoothness of the mixture and prevent segregation of the chalk.

If casein powder is used instead of curd, it has to be stored in water for 3 hours prior to use (320 g casein per 1 litre water). After that, 65 g of Borax is dissolved in 1 litre of hot water, added to the casein mixture and diluted with 12 litres of water.

Clear casein paint coat

If a wipe-resistant finish with the natural colour of the clay render is desired, the required paint coat has to be clear. This can be achieved with a mixture consisting of 1 part non-fat quark and 1.8 to 2 parts water, which is then supplemented by 1/8 to 1/9 part of lime powder. The mixture is sufficient for 20 m² of wall surface and creates a clear to slightly milky satin finish.

Further lime washes with stabilising additives

According to historic sources, mixing lime with liquid manure instead of whey will also lead to a resistant finish. Urea and ammonium acetate increase the strength of china clay (Weiss 1963). This ancient knowledge was already used by the Chinese thousands of years ago: they produced extremely thin china with a clay mixture containing decomposing urine.

A tested and tried version recommends the use of 70 g of animal (bone) glue, which is diluted in half a litre of boiling water and then mixed with 1 kg of lime.

The following additives increase abrasion factor, wipe and weather resistance of lime whitewashes:

- Rye glue made of 15 litres of rye flour and 220 litres of water and some zinc sulfate.
- Agave juice
- Juice of boiled banana leaves
- Juice of prickly pear cactus (opuntia)
- Juice of the candelabra plant (euphorbia lacteal)
- Kapok seed oil
- Linseed oil

Paint coats of non-washable distemper and whitening

Non-washable distemper and whitening paints are only suitable for interior finishes and are not wipe-resistant. For non-washable distemper, a primer coat is required.

Clay flour paint coat

Stir 2 parts of flour (preferably rye flour) in 4 parts of water. After four hours of swelling, the substance is stirred into 3 parts of boiling water and boiled under constant stirring at low heat until it stops swelling. A fraction of the substance is thinned with 2 parts of water, and clay powder, chalk or natural stone dust is continuously added until a smooth mass has formed that can be applied with a brush.

Water-repellent treatment

Interior render in wet rooms or exterior earth render that is supposed to be water-repellent and possess a natural appearance should receive a water-repellent treatment. Due to water-repellent treatments, the moisturising angle of the water drops with respect to the impregnated surface is higher than 90 degrees (refer to figure 8.7). The hydrophobic substance seeps into the pores of the material without sealing them; in other words, it reduces capillary absorbency of the material without dramatically obstructing vapour diffusion. Hydrophobic substances are usually diluted in organic alcohols, hydrocarbons or water.

8.7 Water drop on a non-waterrepellent treated surface (left) and on a water-repellent treated surface (right) (Minke, 2000)

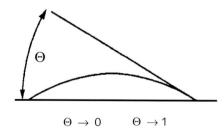

$\Theta \to 0 \qquad \Theta \to 1$

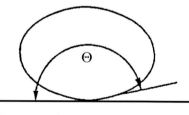

$90° < \Theta < 180° \quad \to \quad \cos \Theta = -\sin (\Theta-90°)$

In the following a few substances that are used as water-repellent treatment:

– Silane or siloxane
– Polysiloxane (silicon resin)
– Siliconate
– Acrylic resin
– Silicic acid ester with water-repellent additives
– Silicates with water-repellent additives

Silane, siloxane and silicon resin chemically react with mineral building materials and are extremely weather-resistant. They reduce water absorption by more than 90 %, but vapour diffusion only by 5 to 8 %.
Acrylic resin and silicic acid ester provide a comparable water resistance, but they also further reduce vapour diffusion.
Due to the varying ingredients of the common brands and since different kinds of earth render react differently to each product, water-repellent treatments should be tested on a sample patch.
The water absorption coefficients (w-values) of the earth-rendered , twice water-repellent treated samples tested at Kassel University range between 0.0 and 0.2 kg/m^{2}h$^{0.5}$.
The water absorption coefficient w denotes the amount of water that is absorbed by a unit area of building material within a specific time.
In a so-called *flooding* procedure, two wet coats of water-repellent treatment are applied in quick succession by means of a roller that is moved downwards along the surface creating a continuous repellent film. The treated surface must be dry and have a temperature not below 8 °C and not above 25 °C. When silane or siloxane is used, the surface should be moist, but not wet. The guidelines of use of the manufacturer have to be observed. After one or more years, the coats can be renewed.

Weather boarding, facing and ventilated cladding

For the protection of straw bale walls, ventilated timber boarding is an effective and simple solution (refer to figure *8.8*). However, this solution also requires the straw bales to be rendered – ideally with a sprayed-on earth render – to comply with fire protection requirements, to prevent nesting of insects and vermin and to increase wind-tightness.
The types of cladding most suitable for this kind of use are conventional or vertical weatherboarding or a cladding of water-tight plywood panels or derived timber products.

8.8 Straw bale wall with ventilated weatherboarding (horizontal and vertical sections)

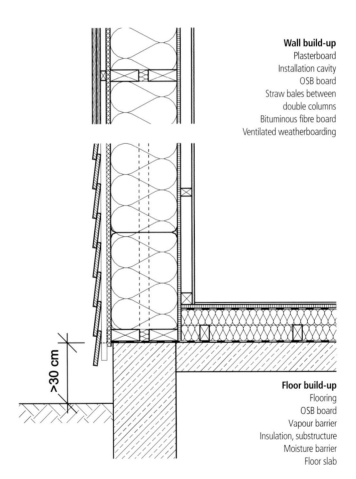

>30 cm

Wall build-up
Plasterboard
Installation cavity
OSB board
Straw bales between
double columns
Bituminous fibre board
Ventilated weatherboarding

Floor build-up
Flooring
OSB board
Vapour barrier
Insulation, substructure
Moisture barrier
Floor slab

9 The building process

9.1 Simple supplementary compaction of straw bales

Supervision and co-ordination on site

Since straw bale building is still relatively unknown, site supervision should be entrusted to an experienced site manager. This encloses efficient job-site mobilisation, monitoring of health and safety regulations and weather protection.

Health and safety measures

Above all, loose straw is a major fire hazard; therefore, the site should be regularly cleaned. Fire extinguishers are a legal requirement and a strict non-smoking policy must be observed.

A first plaster coat should be sprayed on as soon as the wall is erected to provide fire protection.

European law stipulates that "every building site that is set up for a duration of more than 30 working days, that employs more than 20 people, and if work of all employees combined exceeds 500 working days, the appropriate authorities have to be informed two weeks prior to the start of works and a site manager has to be nominated. If procedures on site involve particularly dangerous works, a health and safety plan has to be submitted and its implementation has to be monitored by an authorised health and safety inspector."

Assessment of the quality of the bales

Prior to installation, all bales have to be assessed in regard to their quality. This includes:

– Their moisture contents should not exceed 15 % of the overall weight,
– The straw bales must be highly compressed and possess an apparent density of at least 90 kg/m^3 and
– The strings must be tight and resistant to rotting.

Synthetic strings are more suitable than natural materials. The bales must not contain a large amount of weeds and show no signs of rotting.

Supplementary compaction of the bales

If the straw bales are not sufficiently compressed, that is if their density in dry condition is less than at least 90 kg/m^3, supplementary compaction becomes necessary. This can be conducted in a very simple way as shown in image *9.1*: under imposed weight the strings can be shortened with a toggle that can be pushed into the bale. At the Research Laboratory for Experimental Building at Kassel University, a bale press was built with a car jack so that the bales could be lifted and compacted (*9.2*).

Separating of bales

Often, not the full length of a bale is required but only a part to suit corners, doors or windows. In such an event, bales can be separated and newly tied up with the help of straw bale needles as shown in image 9.4. Needles with handle, tip and eye can be simply manufactured from 6-mm structural steel. The ends of the steel profile can be forged with a hammer into a handle and a flattened tip, which is then sharpened. Into this end the "eye" of the needle of about 4 mm diameter can be drilled and edges should be deburred.

The needles are used to replace the bales' original strings: two equal ends of new string are threaded through the eye of the needle and poked through the bale perpendicular to the original strings (9.4). The new string is then cut – with the needle pulled back out – and both ends are tied. This procedure is repeated for the second original string. After this, the old bale strings can be cut and the bale separated in two parts. The needle should penetrate the bale at the joint between two flakes to enable clean separation of the halves. As shown in picture 9.3, a double-needle can be used to

above 9.2 Apparatus for supplementary compaction of straw bales, developed at the Research Laboratory for Experimental Building at Kassel University

right 9.3 Needles for the separation of bales
9.4 Threading of new strings

Transport and storage

Arms, legs and hands should be protected with appropriate working gear when handling straw bales. Also, a breathing mask should be worn.

Straw bales should be stored on pallets or planks or on a completely dry floor and have to be protected from rain. Bales with a moisture content of more than 15 % are not suitable for construction. Moist bales should be exposed to the wind and stored in rows to dry.

It is advisable to store bales in separate marked stacks according to their length: as building practice has shown, it is very time-consuming to find and repeatedly measure bales of a certain length when they are needed.

9.5 to 9.7

facilitate the entire procedure and determine the distance between strings.

Reshaping of bales

Notches in the bales for columns can be
easily manufactured with a chain saw (9.5).
However, care should be taken not to cut
the strings of the bales.
Bales can be reshaped to suit curved walls.
This can be done as shown in image 9.6, or
by upsetting or alternating the corners as
shown in image 9.7.

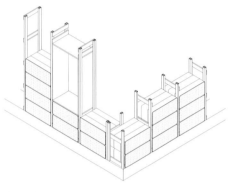

Bale installation

Before the installation of ventilated façade systems, an insect mesh must be fitted (9.8). For load-bearing straw bale walls the position of windows and doors should be marked beforehand, and upright planks should be placed at the corners for support and to check perpendicular wall installation. Usually, bales are laid horizontally in a running bond except if they are stacked snug between framing posts (9.9).

Reinforcing steel rods in the bottom wall layers – as are common in the USA – are not required if the wall is prestressed or stabilised by a post-and-beam structure. These rods can even be a liability as they are thermally coupled to the foundation and may assist condensation within the bales, which may lead to damages.

Wall reinforcement

Load-bearing or free-standing straw bale walls can be reinforced with sharpened bamboo or wooden sticks, which are driven into the bales vertically or at an angle. They should penetrate approximately two and a half bale courses (9.10).

If the straw bales are stacked in front of or behind the timber posts, they should be fixed back to them every other course. Thin vertical bamboo or timber laths that are positioned in pairs on either side of the wall and connected to each other during the stacking process provide a visually attractive reinforcing solution (9.11).

Wall prestressing

Load-bearing straw bale walls need to be prestressed before loads can be imposed. However, prestressing is also advisable for non-loadbearing systems.

To achieve pre-compression for load-bearing structures, a ring beam on top of the walls is required, which is then connected to the foundation with tension ties – for example threaded rods. If tensioned rods are used, they have to be threaded in through the bales, which is time-consuming and requires the rods to be segmented. A simpler method involves tensioned straps, which are fixed to the foundation and tied around the top ring beam (9.12, 9.13) or which are even running below the base slab (see 7.14). Occasionally, the straps may obstruct the rendering of the wall. Additional prestressing might be unneces-

sary altogether if the roof imposes sufficient load onto the walls. This was the case with the test building described in chapter ten: the roof imposed a load of approx. 200 kg/m² and ensured that the walls were prestressed by about 500 kg per metre; thus the wall straps could be removed.
In the case of non-loadbearing systems, it may be useful to assign a double function to inferior purlins: roof support as well as ring beam for the walls (also refer to chapter seven).
The threaded rods and tension ties need to be spaced depending on the required

9.11

9.12 to 9.14

tension, the bending strength of the ring beam and the type of stretching device used – general rules do not apply. In any event, major deformation of the ring beam must be prevented.

The bales of non-loadbearing walls should be stacked starting from the first layer to the one before last and then strapped tight. Finally, the last bale course can be introduced below the inferior purlin/ring beam (9.14) and the straps removed.

Load-bearing straw bale walls can also be prestressed with timber profiles. The profiles are screwed onto the ring beam on top and fixed to the foundation via steel angles with elongated holes. The bales have to be compressed with straps beforehand to ensure that the timber profiles will retain their tension. The timber profiles also provide a good substructure for exterior boarding and interior plaster base.

Removal of deformations

After installation, free-standing or load-bearing straw bale walls may show signs of locally restricted deformation. On most occasions, these can be removed with a mallet or a self-made beater (9.15).

Cropping of bale surfaces

Before rendering a straw bale wall, it may be useful to crop back protruding stalks with a hedge trimmer (*9.17*).

Rendering of the walls

If the wall is to be earth-rendered, a runny undercoat with high clay content should be applied first. This layer should be applied with high pressure and is best sprayed on with a pump. The render should be rather fluid to penetrate a few centimetres beyond the surface immersing all stalks (*9.18*). Stalk ends are smoothed over with a board or a trowel (*9.19*). Image *9.20* shows the under-coat finish in detail.

above 9.16 to 9.17
right 9.18 to 9.19

below 9.20

Back-filling of joints and gaps

Before rendering a straw bale wall, the bales must be smoothed and all cavities and gaps are filled beforehand with loose straw soaked in light clay sludges. The same material can be used to level slight dents (*9.16*).

10 Trial and error – an example

10.1

shop at Kassel University guided by Gernot Minke and Dittmar Hecken. The site of the building is an experimental ground belonging to the Research Laboratory for Experimental Building at Kassel University. In summer 2001, another group of students guided by Gernot Minke and Friedemann Mahlke removed damages and completed the building.

Cost for transport and material amounted to approx. 150 euros per m² usable floor space.

Scheme design

The brief for the experimental structure aimed at the construction of a 36-m² multi-purpose room at minimal cost and using a simple structure that lends itself to do-it-yourself building and environment-friendly building materials.

The objective was to provide a column-free space for seminars, meditation or even sleeping. Loads from the green roof with a 15-cm soil layer and planted with wild weeds and herbs were to be supported only by the walls. Load-bearing straw bale walls require roof loads to be evenly distributed, effectively resulting in a regular geometrical plan – in this case a square was chosen.

Several models were built to find a roof structure suitable for do-it-yourself construction and consisting of round timber profiles (tree trunks). Finally, the plan shown in figure 10.4 was selected as the best solution.

Preliminary note

The test building to be described in the next few paragraphs highlights graphically the many mistakes that can be committed during the planning and construction stages of a straw bale building, the problems that they may cause and how those problems can be solved.

For the test building in question, extreme conditions were deliberately created to test if load-bearing straw bale walls are capable of supporting heavy green roofs (10.1).

The building was conceived and erected by 12 students during the summer of 2000 as part of the "Building with straw bales" work-

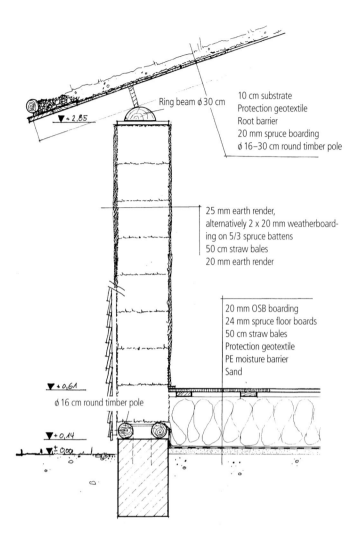

▼ + 2,85

Ring beam ⌀ 30 cm

10 cm substrate
Protection geotextile
Root barrier
20 mm spruce boarding
⌀ 16–30 cm round timber pole

25 mm earth render,
alternatively 2 x 20 mm weatherboarding on 5/3 spruce battens
50 cm straw bales
20 mm earth render

20 mm OSB boarding
24 mm spruce floor boards
50 cm straw bales
Protection geotextile
PE moisture barrier
Sand

▼ + 0,61

⌀ 16 cm round timber pole

▼ + 0,14
▼ ± 0,00

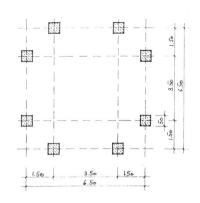

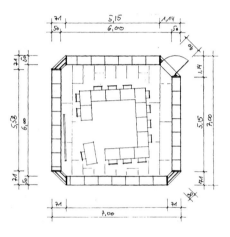

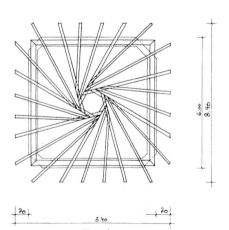

above 10.2
right 10.3 to 10.5
Plan (with desk layout
option for seminars)
Plan of rafters show-
ing ring beam

The roof structure shown in figure *10.5* centres the space in the aesthetically most
pleasing way, and – by means of the central
skylight – the space is well and evenly lit.
The structure itself also benefits from an
exciting interplay of light and shadow.
Three additional full-height windows and
one door at the corners provide additional
lighting. Instead of four strip foundations,
eight point or elephant's feet foundations
with concrete beams supporting the walls
were constructed to save labour and cost.
The beams supporting the walls are continuous beams with equal bending moments
in the middle and at the ends, which leads
only to minimal deflection (refer to figure
10.3). A ring beam consisting of half a 24-
to 28-cm-round timber pole is riding on top
of the walls (*10.7*). Perpendicular boards
have been nailed to the beam to increase

the supporting surface area and structural
interaction with the bales.
An extremely simple low-cost solution was
found for the floor build-up: the ground
was refilled with a 10-cm layer of crushed
rock and compacted with a tamper. This
was covered with a 3-cm layer of sand fol-

lowed by a horizontal moisture barrier (PE foil). Recycled timber pallets serve as ventilated substructure for the straw bales; floating 24-mm OSB boards were laid – without additional battens – directly onto the bales, and the joints were sealed with 25-mm-wide screwed-on OSB strips.

Construction – the first attempt

Construction time needed to be restricted to keep expenditures for weather protection and site security low. Therefore, groups of two to three builders conducted as many preparatory works as possible at the same time: group A removed the grass patches on the ground, stored them for re-use on the green roof, applied the bottom sand layer and compacted it with tampers. Group B prepared the frost-proof foundations that were made of lean concrete supplemented with rocks and coarse gravel to save cement. Group C pre-manufactured the windows

10.10

left 10.9
below 10.12, 10.13,
10.11

and door while group D fabricated the ring beam (*10.7*) and group E peeled and measured the trunks for the roof structure (*10.8*). Meanwhile, group F procured the straw bales from local farmers (*10.9*) and started dividing some of the bales. Thus, all students involved were busy for several days before construction could actually commence. Construction proceeded as follows: first of all, the base beams carrying the walls were positioned on the periodic piers and the gaps closed with boards to prevent mice and insects from nesting there (*10.10*). Next, the windows and the door frames were erected at the corners and fixed to the bottom beams with diagonal braces (*10.11*). For everyone the most satisfactory part of the building process was the installation of the

bales (*10.12*): the walls took shape very quickly and were completed after only one and a half days. Since the bales exercised considerable pressure onto the window frames, they had to be connected with tensioned straps and the window embrasures were reinforced with screwed-on timber battens.

The straw bales were reinforced with sharpened wooden sticks, which were driven diagonnally into the bales, penetrating approximately two and a half bale courses

(*10.13*). The heavy roof rafters were installed manually – so the students-cum-builders had to flex their muscles quite a bit (*10.14* to *10.18*).

The roof consists of nailed timber boarding (*10.19*) and a 2-mm fibrous polyester matting for mechanical protection of the roofing membrane. This is made of PVC-coated polyester fabric whose individual courses were welded together to form a continuous membrane. Sleepers were mounted onto the roof to withstand shear forces of the green roof layer (*10.20*). The roof parapet is formed by a round timber profile which accepts the resulting shear forces from the sleepers and the substrate and is fixed to the rafters via spacers. This creates a slot through which surplus water from the substrate layer can be drained.

A strip of pebbles was placed around the roof perimeter preventing the drainage slot

right 10.21
below from top to bottom
10.20, 10.22

from getting blocked. As a further barrier for soil that might be washed away, grass patches – the ones that were dug out during preparation of the site – were placed on top of the pebbles (*10.21*). For the same reason, grass patches were also placed on top of the sleepers. 50 % of the 16-cm-strong substrate layer consists of pumice, expanded clay and chaff to reduce weight. To accommodate the expected strong compression of the bales, a roof deflection of 25 cm had been allowed for from the beginning. After applying the full load, the roof actually did reach this deflection within several hours. However, unexpectedly the walls buckled to such a degree that collapse of the building seemed immanent and the roof had to be propped up (*10.22*).

The main reason for this failure was the physical constitution of the bales: they were very fresh and were far too moist, they had not been sufficiently compressed. Subsequent measurements showed that the density was only 60–70 kg/m^3.

There were two further structural reasons for the failure: the door opening was wider than the windows. Thus, the bales adjacent to the door received higher loads from the roof than the other bales. Here, deformation was also most severe. A fourth reason is arguably the great slenderness of the 8-bale-high wall, which increases the risk for deformation.

above 10.23 to 10.24
below from left to right
10.25 to 10.27

Solving the problems – the second attempt

Once the errors had been recognized, the team could start tackling them: first of all, every other rafter of the roof was temporarily propped up with scaffolding poles. Subsequently, the roof was slowly lifted with car jacks in steps of 5 cm and the length of the poles was gradually adjusted. This procedure was repeated until the roof had been lifted by about 20 cm and the straw bales could be easily removed (*10.23*).

The bales were then compacted with a self-made bale press and newly tied up (see *9.2*). Hence, the required density of 80–90 kg/m³ could be achieved. Finally, the compacted bales could be re-installed. Additional timber planks of 4/30 cm were posi-

tioned on top of the third and sixth course of bales and in between the window embrasures to improve stability. The boards form a sort of tongue-and-groove connection with the screwed-on timber battens of the embrasures preventing horizontal but allowing vertical movement (*10.24*). Additional thin bamboo sticks were spaced at 40 cm and driven into the bales below the planks to increase friction between planks and bales (*10.24*). After installation of the seventh – final – course, bales were strapped down to achieve maximum pre-stressing/compression (*10.25*).

It resulted in broad straps with a maximum tensile strength of 1,000 kg being required. Thinner straps simply were not suitable to achieve the required pressure. As an alternative method, a heavy truck jack was "wedged" between roof structure and the seventh bale course to compact the bales (*10.26*). The achieved state of compression could then even be secured with thinner straps. Now, the last course of bales could be slid in and the straps removed. The scaffolding poles were gradually winded down until full bearing on the walls had been re-established. This way, buckling of the wall could securely be prevented. Creeping of the bales as a result of the roof loads sub-

above 10.29, 10.28
right 10.30

sided after a few weeks and – after a quick makeover with the hedge trimmer (*10.27*) – the walls could be plastered.

The undercoat was sprayed on with a self-made rendering pump (*10.28*). Clay slurry (*10.29*) was pressurized in a tank and sprayed onto the walls with a hose. Pressure was kept constant at approx. 5 bar by means of a small compressor. After spraying, the walls were smoothed with the hands or with a trowel until all stalks were immersed and levelled. Image *10.30* shows a detailed view of the fairly smooth finish, which is still coarse enough to serve as a plaster base for the second plaster coat.

11 Building cost, insurance, planning permission

Building cost, expenditure of time and personal contribution

There is hardly a universal answer to the question of whether a straw bale building is necessarily less expensive than a conventional house. What kind of building should a straw bale house be compared with and what type of wall construction could one refer to? As a general rule, any comparison should presuppose the same thermal insulation value of the walls. For conventional walls, excellent thermal insulation can only be achieved with considerable expenditures for external thermal insulation composite systems – in this context straw bale walls are definitely less expensive.

In the case of non-loadbearing straw bale walls, cost depends on type and position of the primary structure. A major cost factor is the time-consuming rendering process requiring three coats on either side, with prior filling of gaps and smoothing of the bale surfaces – all of this creates much higher cost than is the case with masonry walls. If the timber posts on the interior are supposed to be exposed and only the infill panels are rendered, plastering works are particularly time-consuming.

Interior cladding with fibrous plasterboard, ordinary plasterboard or derived timber products is less time-consuming and more cost-effective.

A decisive factor for the evaluation of financial viability is the personal contribution of the client and/or his family and friends to the building process. Construction of rendered straw bale walls with a post-and-beam structure may be more time-consuming than rendered masonry walls. Still, their construction may be substantially more economical since even laypersons may conduct building works.

Cost of the straw bales themselves is substantially lower than that of conventional thermal insulation; however, they only represent a small fraction of the overall building cost.

As outlined before, installation and finishing of straw bales as part of walls, roofs and floors are very suitable for do-it-yourself building. Nevertheless, preparation and transport of earth render without professional equipment are extremely time-consuming and should preferably be left to experienced builders with the required equipment. However, the client can install wall cladding or apply paint and varnish coats to the render himself, which may lead to substantial savings.

Insurance of building

As far as fire-protected or fully rendered straw bale walls with an F90 (90 minutes) fire rating are concerned (refer to chapter six), insurance of the building against fire is unproblematic. The building would have to be classified as a solid construction. Insurance against damages by water pipes or floods might be a more complicated issue, as drainage of a soaked straw bale wall is expensive and labour-intensive. It is important to have the insurance acknowledge the particular type of wall structure so that in the event of damage it cannot refuse payment.

Planning permission

In many countries, both load-bearing and non-loadbearing straw bale structures are officially permitted. Various states in the USA have passed particular regulations for straw bale building stipulating the maximum moisture content of the bales, minimal wall thickness, maximum loading of the walls and finishing treatments. The most detailed regulations are the California Straw Bale Code (see King 1996, page 142 et seqq.) and the Arizona Straw Bale Building Code (see Magwood & Mack 2002, page 219 et seqq.)

In Denmark, France, Great Britain, the Netherlands, Ireland and Switzerland, planning permission for straw bale buildings has been granted in the past.

In Ship Harbour in Nova Scotia, Canada, even a two-storey building with load-bearing straw bale walls was permitted (see Magwood & Mack 2002, page 199 et seqq.).

Another two-storey building with load-bearing straw bale walls was permitted and built in Disentis, Switzerland (refer to Part II, page 96–97).

II Built examples in detail

This chapter introduces buildings from all over the world to highlight the great variety of structural solutions and design that can be found in straw bale building. Construction with straw bales has mostly been practiced by private clients, which explains why the majority of featured projects are private residences. Recently, however, a number of larger buildings unrelated to single-family use, such as schools, offices, information centres and even factory halls have been erected; a selection of such projects is equally presented here.

Residential building in Ouwerkerk, Zeeland, the Netherlands

The Butterfly House by Jan Sonneveld was the first building to receive planning permission in the Netherlands. The client had already made provisions with an architect friend for a conventional building when he heard about straw bale building and changed his plans. Since the architect was inexperienced in straw bale building, the project caused a lot of hassle and the budget was consequently exceeded by 200,000 euros (although the straw bales had only cost 500 euros!).

The shape and particular design of the building caused considerable cost. The envisaged butterfly shape is very appealing in itself and renders the building an eye-catcher. However, the small radiuses on the corners proved unsuitable for the chosen type of construction. Bending of the bales for the "Oval Office" – that was supposed to be load-bearing – was practically impossible, so a supplementary timber frame had to be introduced.

The building possesses a primary steel structure and a roofing of trapezoid metal sheet. At the beginning, this solution had appeared very straightforward, but during construction under the conditions of straw bale building it resulted in complicated details and thermal bridges that had to be resolved. Cost was further increased due to the lack of efficient coordination of all parties and proper working drawings. This caused delay and many things had to be improvised. The fact that local contractors did not conduct work on the roof properly added to the difficulties: the roof overhang had been constructed too short, causing many problems with the exterior render as a result of the rainy conditions during summer. Since the first attempt to produce a weather-proof exterior fabric with lime render failed, eventually earth render with a multiple lime-casein whitewash provided the most sensible solution.

An approximately 1-m-tall cavity lime-sand-stone wall with core insulation supports the structure. The floor rests on a thick layer consisting of seashells and expanded clay. Due to its exceptional shape that was realised by use of straw bales, the building received nationwide acclaim and the broader public could be introduced to straw bale building. (*II.1* to *II.6*)

above II.2
left page II.1

Design: Wim van Dort, Jan Sonneveld
Straw bale works: Martin Oehlmann
Wall system: main building: steel frame
with straw bale infill panels,
"Oval Office": load-bearing straw bale walls
with supplementary timber structure
Completion: 1998
Living/Floor area: approx. 200 m^2

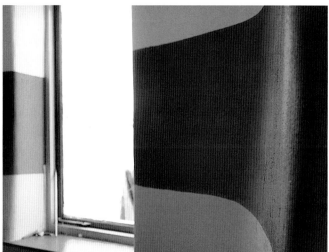

■ Residential building in Balneario Punta Ballena, Uruguay

Wall and roof structure of the building consist of eucalyptus trunks. In front of the primary timber structure runs a facing 50-cm-thick non-loadbearing straw bale wall supported by a base wall of local natural stone.

On the interior and exterior the straw bales are rendered with two coats of earth render. The 2-cm-strong undercoat consists of earth with chaff aggregate; the 5-mm-strong finishing coat is a lean earth render (earth-sand ratio 1:4) containing earth with high clay content that was found on site. The 12-cm-strong partitions are made of basketwork and are earth-rendered on both sides. The roof is thatched with a 25-cm layer of reed. (*II.7* to *II.8*)

Design: Cecilia Alderton
Completion: 1997
Living/Floor area: approx. 100 m²

II.7

II.8

right II.10, II.11

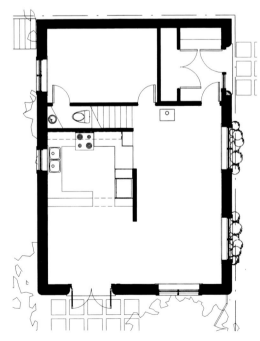
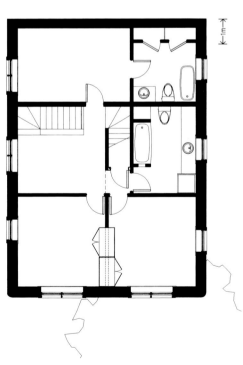

■ Residential building in central Montreal, Canada

With the construction of a straw bale house on a split block, within ten minutes walking distance from downtown Montreal, the architect pursued a number of objectives: firstly, it was to be demonstrated that houses on small sites increase the availability of residential urban space and facilitate the financing of such projects. Furthermore, a building type was reintroduced into the neighbourhood that strongly resembled the historical building fabric. Another goal was the introduction of straw bale building into an urban context, here into the large Canadian cities.

The design process had to be conducted in close consultation with the local authorities since neither rendered façades nor pitched roofs complied with local building regulations – although they exactly followed many historical examples.

above II.12
right II.13

The house consists of a timber frame with straw insulation in the floor and walls. The floor slabs themselves are concrete slabs that were merely waxed and varnished.
The bales in the exterior walls were installed vertically between the timber posts. The bales are positioned far enough inside to form a continuous surface outside that was finished with lime-cement render (ratio 5:1). The interior posts are clad with expanded metal preventing cracking of the render. The roof consists of a zinc-clad steel structure that was insulated with cellulose – and not, as originally planned, with straw bales. The partitions do not consist of the common plywood panels but of natural resin-based boards with straw chaff aggregate. (*II.9* to *II.13*)

Design: Julia Bourke
Site supervision: Michel Bergeron / Julia Bourke
Wall system: ballon frame with straw bale infill
Completion: 1999
Living / Floor area: 186 m²

■ Prefabricated single-family home in Hitzendorf, near Graz, Styria, Austria

The two-storey family home in Hitzendorf is a prefabricated wooden post-and-beam structure filled with straw bales. The prefab elements have a diagonal boarding and are assembled just like any other prefab house. The floor slab on top of the basement – which was built conventionally – consists of straw bale insulated prefabricated panels with OSB boarding on either side.

The roof is a conventional structure; however, it received a 4-cm-thick interior boarding to provide an F30 fire rating, and the cavities between the rafters are filled with straw bales. This is also the case with the intermediate floor slab.

The walls are based on a 75-cm structural grid and have a vapour and a wind barrier on either side, respectively. The exterior and interior trass-lime render was applied on top of reed matting.

This building system benefits from the same advantages as conventional prefab buildings: they can be erected fast and simply. Nevertheless, the rigid structural grid tends to cause problems since it does not suit the varying lengths and irregular edges of the bales. Therefore, the prefabrication process requires quite a bit of additional manual work to avoid potential thermal bridges. (II.14 to II.21)

Design: Strohtec
Consulting: ASBN
Wall system: prefabricated timber structure with straw core insulation
Completion: 1999
Living/Floor area: approx. 135 m^2

above from top to bottom
II.14 Delivery of wall elements
II.15 Installation of floor slab
II.16 Completed floor slab

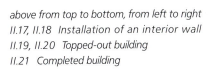
above from top to bottom, from left to right
II.17, II.18 Installation of an interior wall
II.19, II.20 Topped-out building
II.21 Completed building

■ Single-family home in Dobersdorf, Burgenland, Austria

This family home in Dobersdorf, Burgenland, has a prominent diagonal pitched roof conceived in reaction to the particular local situation, which prevented direct north-south orientation of the building.

The layout achieves the largest possible glazed area permitted by the given site boundaries. Different areas – the large south-facing winter garden, the central living areas and the north-facing supplementary spaces – zone the building along an imaginary line from warm to cooler spaces. The building's services also follow a simple concept: the electrical wires are screened from electromagnetic radiation; they are few in numbers and the circuit includes so-called demand (or "Bio") switches. Water piping was kept as short as possible to restrict heat losses. The entire building is heated by a central tiled stove.

The walls consist of a timber frame structure with exterior larch weatherboarding and interior diagonal boarding creating a 20-cm-wide cavity. On the inside, in front of the diagonal boarding, sits a non-loadbearing straw bale wall, which was rendered with earth on either side. Placing the bales inside of the primary structure creates a homogeneous surface, which also facilitates subsequent finishing work. A disadvantage is the resulting great wall thickness. The described structure is based on the idea that condensate can dry off more easily in the air cavity and that repairs on the walls can be conducted more conveniently.

The straw bale wall received an interior earth render coat. Products like OSB and plasterboard were ruled out to enable vapour diffusion through the wall. The roof was insulated with a 36-cm layer of cellulose fibre.

In the back garden, a shed with a reversed wall build-up was built: here, the primary structure was positioned inside to facilitate fixing of hooks and shelving. The earth render was mixed with 50 % cow dung to make it weather-resistant. (*II.22* to *II.26*)

from top to bottom
II.22, II.23

Design: Gerald Harbusch (Client)

Straw bale works: Gerald Harbusch

Wall system: timber post-and-beam structure
with straw bale insulation

Completion: 2000

Living/Floor area: 150 m^2

*above from top
to bottom II.24, II.25
right II.26*

II.27

II.28

Urban cottage in Berkeley, California, USA

This one-bedroom cottage is located in a relatively dense urban context, adjacent to apartment buildings. Built into the backyard of an existing house, the zoning restrictions called for a rectangular plan with the short side facing south. The project was a challenging task in terms of passive solar design and, due to the restricted allowable area, a tough call concerning the question of whether to use thick bale walls.

The open kitchen, dining and living area on the first floor are invigorated by a greenhouse window over the stairwell, which captures the afternoon light. Bedroom, bath and a small study are on the second floor. The thick straw bale wall turned out to be a good device to create a sense of intimacy, cosiness and security. By carefully responding to sight lines, the space feels sunny and open, while neighbours' views do not get past the deep window jambs. Another asset is the excellent sound insulation of straw bale walls.

For solar gains, the house ended up having large openings on the narrow southern gable end. Due to the difficult situation near a major seismic fault line, this could only be solved by steel X-bracing of the wood post-and-beam structure. The passive solar performance of the cottage got revealed in this little anecdote: a hydronic heating system got put into exposed slab for backup heat in the winter, but the plumbing did not get put together properly and did not work. However, living there for three years, the owner has never felt the need to fix the problem, since the house remains comfortable without any mechanical heating. (II.27 to II.31)

Design: DSA Architects – Dan Smith, Dietmar Lorenz
Owner/Builder: Eugene DeChristopher
Wall system: post-and-beam construction, straw bale walls
Living/Floor area: 88 m²

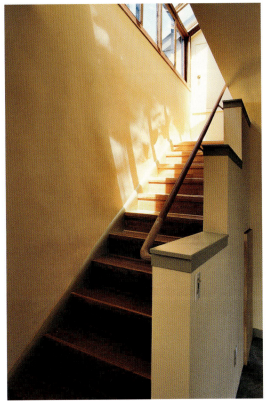

from top
to bottom II.29, II.30
left II.31

II.32

Single-family home in Bryson, North Carolina, USA

The small town of Bryson City at the edge of the Great Smoky Mountains National Park in North Carolina was an ideal place for building with and within nature. The completed three-storey straw bale building nestles neatly into the mountainous environment and is ideal for various outdoor activities of the clients and the travel business they operate.

The building comprises non-loadbearing straw bale walls with primary timber structure. As is still the custom in the US, chicken wire was introduced into the render of the straw bales, which is believed to increase the strength of the render. But rather the contrary is the case: the wire obstructs movements of the structure, thus assisting the formation of cracks and fissures. (II.32 to II.35)

Design: Sustainable Structures, New Zealand
Straw bale works: Bill Green
Wall system: timber frame with straw infill panels
Completion: 2001
Living/Floor area: approx. 220 m²

 II.33

II.34

II.35

II.36

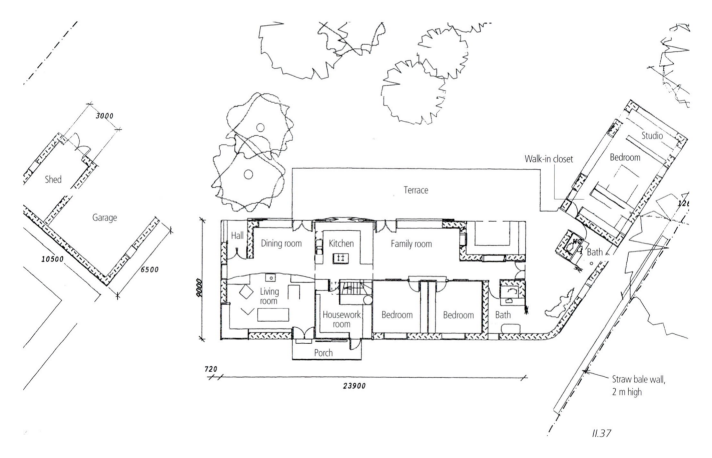

Shed

3000

Garage

10500

6500

Hall

Dining room

Kitchen

Family room

Terrace

Walk-in closet

Studio

Bedroom

Bath

Living room

Housework room

Bedroom

Bedroom

Bath

Porch

720

23900

Straw bale wall,
2 m high

II.37

■ Single-family home with guest house, games room and garage in Galston, near Sydney, Australia

The house is located in the Sydney suburb of Galston amidst a eucalyptus forest and bush area, which counts among the zones in Australia that are highly threatened by bush fires. Even in such zones, planning permission for straw bale buildings is not a big issue any more since rendered straw bales have passed the respective CSIRO (Commonwealth Scientific & Industrial Research Organisation) bush fire tests. Overall cost ranged around AUS $ 1,3 million (750,000 euros) that was partly financed with bank loans.

The layout represents a group of four buildings – the main building, the garage, a games room bordering on a tennis court and a guest wing. The latter was built first and offered accommodation to the entire family during construction. A permaculture garden as well as active and passive use of solar energy are part of the general concept. On the premises, surplus energy is produced that can be sold back to the local energy grid.

The buildings are single-storey, only the main building comprises a central loft providing additional living and playing area. The layout of the bathrooms of the main and guest buildings is particularly interesting in terms of design: in conjunction with a curved straw bale wall, they form a courtyard. Both bathrooms can be fully opened towards this courtyard.

All windows were placed relatively far outside, producing deep interior embrasures, which were rounded (refer to figure 7.32). The buildings consist of a timber frame structure with straw bale infill panels. The interior wall faces are finished with earth, the exterior faces with lime. The earth render of the guest wing was mixed with cow dung. The client insisted that all walls be constructed perfectly straight. This way, the wall finishes cannot be distinguished from a plasterboard partition.

Floor slabs and interior partitions were made from 55-mm boards of pressed straw which are self-supporting, so the timber structure could be reduced to a minimum. Throughout the building recycled timber was used from the demolished building that had existed on the site before. (II.36 to II.39)

*from top to bottom
II.38, II.39*

Design: Andrea Wilson
Straw bale works: Frank Thomas
Wall system: timber post-and-beam structure with straw bale infill panels
Completion: 2001
Living/Floor area: approx. 450 m^2
(Main building 250 m^2, games room 64 m^2, guest wing 70 m^2, garage 65 m^2)

Single-family home in Lower Lake, California, USA

This house for a non-medical practitioner in Northern California is largely a do-it-your-self construction. After being designed by the architects, it was built with the help of friends, acquaintances and a few hired hands within one year. It nestles into a 13-acre site covered with oak trees and is the first earth-rendered straw bale building that received planning permission in California. The client – a female artist working with ceramics – seized the opportunity to design every single room individually, using paint coats with natural pigments in addition to the earth and lime render. The house is orientated according to passive solar principles and possesses highly efficient cellulose insulation; thus, hardly any additional heating is required. A cooling tower and large roof overhangs (shading) keep the building cool during summer; under-floor heating and a little stove can bridge supply shortfalls during winter. Connection to the public supply grid was not necessary since hot water and electricity are produced with solar energy.
(II.40 to II.43)

Design: Pete Gang and Kelly Lerner,
One World Design
Site supervision: client
Wall system: rice straw insulated and
rendered timber structure
Completion: 2001
Living/Floor area: approx. 148 m²

II.40

II.41

II.42

II.43

above II.44, II.45
right II.46

Single-family home in Lake Biwa, Japan

The house situated at Lake Biwa, Japan's largest lake, is one of the first buildings in Japan that use rice straw for the insulation of walls.

Straw bales were used for the walls on the ground floor while reed was used for the upper floor and the roof; the latter was clad with derived timber boards.

The straw bales were rendered, employing various traditional techniques: for the exterior render Tosasshikkui was used. This is a lime-earth finish with added straw, which is supposed to minimise cracking. In the entrance hall, Kakiotoshi was chosen – an earth-straw mix that was keyed with a steel brush and results in a rustic Japanese interior. In the kitchen, the slightly shimmering earth finish – Otsumigaki – was achieved by polishing the still wet render with a smooth trowel or stones. (*II.44* to *II.50*)

Design: Goichi Oiwa (Seian University of Art and Design)
Wall system: timber structure with rice straw bale insulation, reed insulation on top floor
Completion: 2003
Living/Floor area: 140 m^2

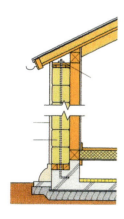

1F

2F

from top to bottom and left to right II.47, II.48, II.49, II.50

■ The Spiral House, Castlebar, County Mayo, Ireland

The Spiral House is one of Europe's first load-bearing straw bale buildings to receive planning permission and the very first two-storey building of its kind with official permission in Europe. This project was developed as one attempt to present an alternative to today's global economy that destroys nature and seriously damages humanity. The house was almost entirely built by freelance workers and with the support of Amazon Nails, a predominantly female project developer. Amazon Nails promotes the idea of a self-conducted building process that incorporates laypersons and rethinks the erection of a building as a shared experience in which everyone can participate according to his or her abilities. Just like the building process, the design was governed by these principles. Client and designer Norita Clesham based her plan on the shape of a Nautilus shell. It is open to the outside, but at the same time creates a sense of protection and security by means of the contracting interior. The load-bearing walls were erected on a foundation of local limestone. As a result of the complicated roof shape, the rafters (timber H-profiles) range between lengths of 3.5 m to 8.5 m; the central chimney supports them. The roof covering consists of approximately 7,000 handmade cedar shingles.

The straw bale walls received two earth undercoats and then three topcoats of lime render. The finishing coat had to be reapplied and repaired several times because it had been destroyed by frost: rendering had been left late, which prevented carbonating of the render and allowed water to penetrate the finish. (*II.51* to *II.54*)

II.52

II.53

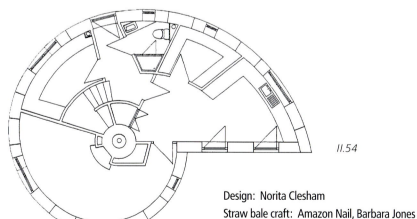

II.54

Design: Norita Clesham
Straw bale craft: Amazon Nail, Barbara Jones
Wall system: two-storey load-bearing walls
Completion: 2002
Living/Floor area: approx. 110 m^2

left page II.51

■ Load-bearing straw bale house in Disentis, Switzerland

The load-bearing straw bale building situated in the Swiss Alps on an altitude of 1,300 m has a clean and simple shape derived from the straw bale dimensions. Jumbo bales, 1.2 m wide, were used to achieve very low energy consumption and to handle extreme snow loads of up to 650 kg/m^2. For better structural analysis of the building, loading tests were conducted beforehand: imposed loads of 3 to 6 tons established that bales of 74 cm height would creep (deflect) by 7 cm. These findings were incorporated into the design of walls and south-west timber-glass façade. The floor slab is a stacked plank floor supported by the straw bales. The roof is composed of trussed girders and a thermal insulation consisting of two layers of small bales.

The walls were rendered with lime-cement plaster on top of a wire mesh. As a result of the sloping site, the building rests on concrete pylons. If required, they can be enclosed by masonry in the future to create storage and workshops.

The load-bearing building received planning permission without being deferred by the authorities. In Southern Tyrol, Italy, the construction of a three-storey load-bearing building with Jumbo bales is scheduled for 2004. (*II.55* to *II.58*)

Ground floor plan

First floor plan

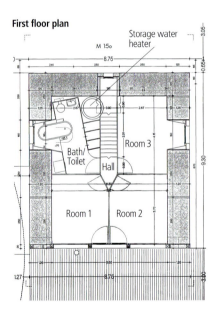

from top to bottom
II.55, II.56, II.57

Scheme design: Werner Schmidt
Site supervision: Werner Schmidt
Wall system: load-bearing Jumbo bales
(74 x 125 x 250 cm)
Completion: 2002
Living/Floor area: 110 m^2

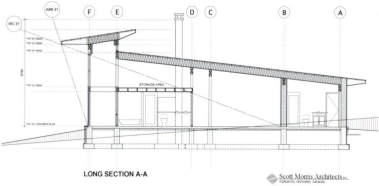

LONG SECTION A-A

Scott Morris Architects inc.
TORONTO, ONTARIO, CANADA

above II.59
left II.60
right page from
top to bottom
II.61, II.62

■ Passive house in Cavan, Ontario, Canada

In 1998, the client's family decided to buy a 100-acre piece of land in Cavan, Ontario, to escape urban life with its noise, traffic and pollution. Two thirds of the land consist of forest, the rest are meadows, bush and swamps.

The proposed residential building was supposed to be built from "healthy" materials and be independent of the local energy and sewage grid. To achieve this goal, the design had to ensure excellent thermal insulation and very low energy consumption of the house.

The house was orientated according to passive solar principles, with the south façade being nearly fully glazed and the other three façades nearly fully solid. Since the roof is rising towards the south, the sun can penetrate deeply into the building during winter and heat up the concrete floor slab. A large roof overhang provides sufficient shading during summer. Thus, the building can almost entirely do without supplementary heating or cooling. Under-floor heating provides heat during long cold periods with little sunshine. Since this system uses electrical power, it is to be supplemented by an efficient wood stove in the future. The electrical energy for household use is entirely produced out of wind and solar energy and is stored in power cells. The client developed LED luminaires for the lighting of the building, as LEDs use very little power but are still very hard to find as a complete lighting system. A propane gas cooker is used in the kitchen. Propane gas is also used for supplementary heating of pre-heated service water from solar tanks. This way, the household is virtually independent of the local supply grid.

The building consists of a timber post-and-beam structure with exposed interior posts. The straw bales have been rendered on both sides with cement. The interior topcoat is a mixture of earth render and white marble powder. The walls are protected from rain by large roof overhangs. The roof was

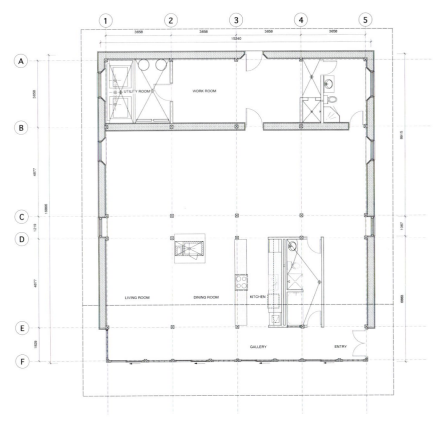

insulated with a particular rockwool produced from recycled materials: it is fire-resistant and maintains its full thermal insulation properties even when it is moist. (*II.59* to *II.62*)

Design: Scott Morris Architects
Site supervision: Camel's Back Construction
Straw bale works: Herwig van Soom
Wall sytem: timber frame with straw bale facing wall
Completion: 2004
Living/Floor area: approx. 250 m²

II.63

II.64

■ First straw bale house in Vienna, Austria

This project is about the supplementary fit-out and raising of an existing backyard building in a densely populated district of Vienna. The building's ground floor was already used as a garage; the upper floor could be fitted out for residential use. The design is based on economical considerations and efficient sourcing of materials: the project was to be realised as low-cost and environmentally friendly as possible. Due to the particular backyard situation, the design had to ensure attractive views for the users and, at the same time, prevent undesired infringement of the their privacy. This could be achieved by a number of measures like low eaves with a large roof overhang providing visual and solar protection. A planted balcony in front of the generous glazing visually enlarges the living area.

The building itself can be accessed from a forecourt on the ground floor. As a first step during construction, the old roof and – as far as required – the old compartment walls and chimneys were demolished. To the remaining parts of the compartment walls an interior timber structure was added. The walls and floors were insulated with cellulose and the roof with straw bales. Thorough design and construction ensured that the project – apart from the creation of additional living space – also managed to improve the spatial quality of the courtyard with the raising of the existing building and the introduction of supplementary green space. The chosen building method ensured very low building cost of approx. 900 euros/m^2 despite the complexity of the task. (*II.63* to *II.67*)

Design: Karen Allmer, Florian Macke
Wall system: existing solid structure, cellulose-insulated timber frame, roof structure insulated with straw bales
Completion: 2003
Living/Floor area: 180 m^2

from top to bottom
II.65, II.66

II.67

■ Single-family home in Blanden, Belgium

The two-storey straw bale building near Brussels was designed by the architect as a home for his family. The roof with simple metal sheeting is detached from the rest of the building and provides merely weather protection. This way, a roof terrace affording panoramic views of the entire surroundings could be created. The detached roof and lightweight southern façade creates a contrasting effect with the solid straw bale walls.

The building is organised on two levels: the "daytime level" on the ground floor and the "night-time level" on the first floor. The load-bearing structure consists of 8.5-m-tall round timber profiles on a 3 m x 4 m grid. On three sides, non-loadbearing facing straw bale walls were positioned in front of the primary structure. The southern façade consists of large glazed areas and insulated timber infill panels.

The walls were rendered on both sides with a mixture of loam and chaff; uneven patches were not levelled but rather traced and expressed. However, despite the large roof overhang, the earth render showed first signs of erosion on the weather side after one year. (*II.68* to *II.70*)

above II.68
left II.69
below II.70

Design: Herwig van Soom
Straw bale works: Herwig van Soom
Wall system: timber structure out of round profiles with non-loadbearing straw bale facing wall
Completion: 2002
Living/Floor area: approx. 135 m^2

Low-energy house in Maria Laach, Austria

At the beginning, this family home had been planned as a conventional timber structure with cellulose insulation. Only during construction, after completion of the basement, the clients decided to use straw bale insulation, which could also be sourced from the farm of the parents. The decision was triggered by the client's participation in a symposium on straw bale building. The primary structure had to be slightly adjusted to suit the large wall thickness of the straw bales even though they were installed vertically: the thickness, of 35 cm still exceeds the usual dimensions. To achieve this thickness, the posts were doubled up in pairs of 4/14 cm. The gap of 7 cm was filled with cork insulation, resulting in a thermally separated system without thermal bridges that can usually only be achieved with wooden H-profiles. Hence, the wall structure, if regarded as an isolated system, meets passive house standards. The roof structure was doubled up in a similar fashion to suit the new insulation – the existing dimension of the rafters of 20 cm was increased to 34 cm.
On the inside, the exterior wall received diagonal boarding for reinforcement and a facing wall of earth-straw bricks providing the required thermal mass for indoor temperature and air-humidity control.
On the exterior, the wall was finished with mineral render that was applied to ventilated cement fibreboard. This finish was a result of local planning regulations and so the building is no longer recognisable as a straw bale house. (*II.71* to *II.74*)

Design: BM. Winfried Schmelz
Site supervision: Raiffeisen-Lagerhaus
Wall system: lightweight timber construction with straw bale insulation on basement
Completion: 2003
Living / Floor area: 230 m^2

II.71

II.72

above II.73
below II.74

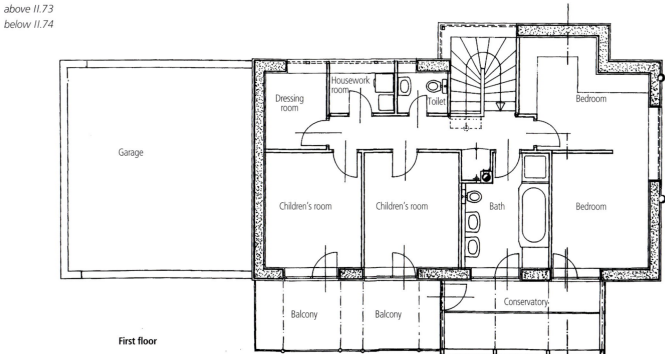

Garage

Dressing room

Housework room

Toilet

Bedroom

Children's room

Children's room

Bath

Bedroom

Balcony

Balcony

Conservatory

First floor

Passive house in Wienerherberg, Austria

The building – designed as a passive house – has a cubic, modernist appearance and arguably would not immediately be identified as a classic straw bale building. The building faces southwards; a large roof overhang provides sufficient shading during summer.

As it is located near a brook, the designers decided to elevate the ground floor 1 m above ground level and support the entire building on strip foundations so that the timber structure would not touch the ground. The building itself was prefabricated and the straw insulated framed timber elements received an exterior larch weatherboarding. Interior finishes are plasterboard and earth-rendered structural boards that also comply with the required F30 fire rating. Thus, building cost of 1,100 euros/m^2 and an annual energy use of 12 kWh/m^2 could be achieved. Energy is provided by a heat pump connected to the air-conditioning. (*II.75* to *II.77*)

II.75

II.76

Design: BM. Winfried Schmelz

Site supervision: Zimmerei Proksch-Weilguni

Wall system: prefabricated timber frame, straw bale insulation

Completion: 2004

Living/Floor area: 151 m^2

II.78

II.79

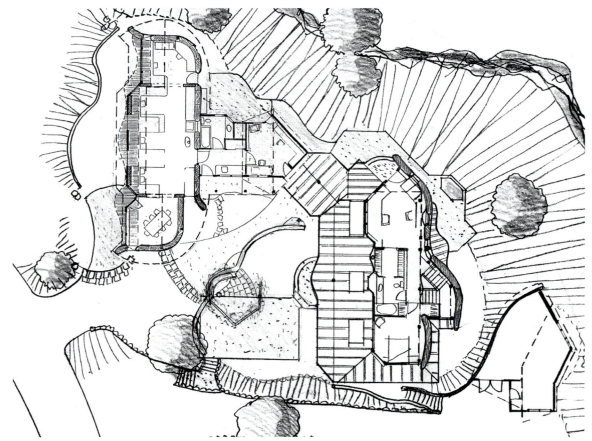

II.80

■ Trout Farm Complex, Tassaraja Canyon, California, USA

Trout Farm is the home of the San Luis Sustainability Group – a design practice specialising in the planning and construction of sustainable buildings and compounds since 1976. The group attaches great importance to multi-disciplinary cooperation with other research groups.

The compound comprises a design studio, a residential building and a workshop and was built in various stages over a period of eight years. The simple handling and modelling capability of straw bales gave rise to the idea to reflect the natural environment in the architecture. Hence, an organic irregular structure was designed in contrast to the common straight and rectangular buildings.

The buildings are partly built with load-bearing walls and partly with timber post-and-beam structures with vertical straw bale infill panels. The roofs consist of a timber structure with metal cladding; two roofs have been insulated with cellulose, one with straw bales and one with "aircrete" – extremely lightweight expanded concrete. The walls have been rendered with earth without the use of any vapour barriers or supplementary paint coats. Large roof overhangs and a drainage system protect the building from rain and entering water. (II.78 to II.82)

Design: Ken Haggard, Polly Cooper
Straw bale works: Scott Clark
Wall system: partly load-bearing, partly primary timber frame with straw infill panels
Completion: 1996 (office), 1997 (residential building), 2002 (workshop)
Living/Floor area: 327 m^2 (office 140 m^2, residential 140 m^2, workshop 47 m^2)

II.81

II.82

■ Residential and office building in London, United Kingdom

The residential and office building is situated at the end of a street in a former industrial estate of London, hemmed in between rail tracks and small Victorian railway cottages. One leg of the L-shaped building houses an office, the other accommodates the residential wing. A room that can equally be used as meeting room and dining room links the two wings. The five-storey tower establishes the building as a visible landmark.

Strictly speaking, the building is not a pure straw bale structure, as straw bales were not used consistently throughout the building; instead, a mix of various building methods and materials was chosen. However, all methods ensured that materials came from sustainable sources and that their incorporated energy was low. Hence, recycled concrete was used just as well as sand bags filled with cement, lime and sand: the mixture will harden over time and – as the organic textile fibres decompose – it will reveal a coarse concrete finish.

The sleeping area was insulated with straw bales sitting between latticed timber posts. They are visible between the polycarbonate cladding, which is ventilated to ensure that condensation will not damage the bales. By means of this constructional device, the straw bales could be exposed and protected at the same time. On the inside, the straw bales are lime-rendered. The type of insulation used ensures that the heating period for these spaces is restricted to just a few weeks during winter. (*II.83* to *II.89*)

Design and site supervision: Sarah Wigglesworth
Straw bale works: Scott Clark
Wall system: partly load-bearing, partly primary timber frame with straw infill panels
Completion: 2001
Living area: 264 m²
Office area: 210 m²

II.84

II.85

*from top to bottom
left to right II.86, II.87,
II.88, II.89*

112 ■ Built examples in detail

Ulenkrug Farm, Stubbendorf, Mecklenburg-West Pomerania, Germany

The Ulenkrug Farm is an agricultural cooperative, founded in 1995, that grows organic crops on approximately 42 ha. It currently hosts a permanent community of 18 adults and nine children. The community is based on the ideas brought about by the French apprentices' movement Longo Maï, a Provençal phrase, which means, "Long may it last". These cooperatives promote an alternative economic and social approach to agriculture and handcrafts. Besides the production of organic food, the Ulenkrug Farm seeks to advance cultural and social variety linked with social commitment. The farm-owned shop supplies customers in Berlin and the Mecklenburg region, and products are exchanged with other Longo Maï cooperatives. Based on the old apprentice tradition, many Longo Maï buildings are constructed with the assistance of journeymen. In this way, qualified labour could be resourced to erect the timber structure for the new community building. The trees for the traditional timber-framed building were felled one year before construction began. The straw bales were sourced from a neighbouring farm, which also helped to restrict transport distances.

The straw bales are stacked vertically as a free-standing wall in front of the timber structure. Already at base-build stage, the substructure for the exterior timber cladding was fixed to the primary structure with timber profiles, which also provided the required stability for the straw bale wall. The wall received an additional exterior earth render coat to provide wind-tightness. The interior timber frame compartments were filled with lightweight loam and a partial solar wall heating was installed.
(*II.90* to *II.92*)

Design: Walter Lack
Site supervision: self-management
Wall system: framed timber structure with non-loadbearing straw bale facing wall
Completion: 2004
Living/Floor area: approx. 400 m^2

from top to bottom
II.90, II.91, II.92

Design: Achim Wüst

Site supervision: Axel Linde

Wall system: wooden post-and-beam structure
with non-loadbearing straw bale facing wall

Completion: 2002

Living area: 110 m^2

II.93

■ Residential building for ethnic German resettlers, Wargoldshausen, Lower Franconia, Germany

The two-storey residential building in Lower Franconia was the first of its kind to receive planning permission and to be built in Germany. It offers 400 m² of living area on a footprint of 11 x 21 m. The building forms part of a farm for ethnic German resettlers that is based on sustainable principles such as organic farming, including crops and life stock; decentralised power and water supply; and a phyto-purification plant (sewage treatment with plants). The straw bales for construction were resourced from the farm itself.

The building is a post-and-beam structure which is supported on point foundations. The ground floor is entirely ventilated, so that moisture cannot penetrate the straw bales, which were also used as insulation material for floors and roof. The double-height straw bale walls are up to 8 m tall and are earth-rendered on both sides: the exterior face received an earth undercoat with two top coats of stored wet lime with integrated jute matting. Finally, the still moist render was finished with a triple-pigmented lime whitewash.

The straw bales were positioned in front of the primary timber structure to achieve maximum air-tightness.

The roof consists of two levels. The lower level is part of the space enclosure and supports the straw bales; the upper level is a green roof.

As an additional measure to the projecting roof protecting the tall walls, a canopy runs around the building's perimeter above the ground floor. (II.93 to II.96)

from top to bottom
II.94, II.95, II.96

The Woodage Sawmill, Mittagong, Australia

The Woodage is a Southern Australian enterprise processing certified timber according to FSC (Forest Stewardship Council) directives. In cooperation with the WWF, the FSC awards a seal of approval, binding the certified company to certain standards of sustainable forestry, but also, for instance, to observance of the rights of indigenous communities. The Woodage was the first certified company in Australia and was a supplier for the Olympic Village construction sites in Sydney.

The building houses a mixture of sawmill and joinery with a number of attached offices and a show and sales room. Building cost ranged around AUS $ 1.1 million (640,000 euros), 50 % of which was financed by banks.

The building consists of a steel skeleton; at the two narrow sides, the compartments were filled with straw bales and received a lime render. The rear wall of the building is 52 m long and 4.8 m tall. An expansion joint was required in the middle and prevents cracking and fissures. A 1.3-m roof overhang and a veranda protect the weather side. External bamboo pinning provides additional reinforcement to the long external wall.

Office and sales room are separated from the hall by another straw bale wall, which provides excellent sound insulation against machine noises form the production hall. (*II.97* to II.*101*)

Design: Van der Ryn Architects
Design team: David Arkin, Bruce King
Wall system: timber-concrete structure, rice straw infill panels
Completion: 1996
Floor area: approx. 460 m^2

from top to bottom
II.100, II.101

above II.102
left II.103
right page from top
to bottom II.104,
II.105

▪ Straw bale dome as a rehearsal and performance space in Forstmehren, Westerwald, Germany

In Forstmehren in the Westerwald region near Frankfurt, a straw bale dome was built for the musician and composer Thomas Kagermann as a studio and performance space.

The circular interior has a clear diameter of 8.2 m and a clear height of approx. 5.1 m. A 2.7-m-wide window opens the structure towards the south, affording views of the surrounding meadows and fields. A triple-layered acrylic skylight with a diameter of 1.8 m provides well-balanced central lighting.

On the inside, the vault has been finished with a triple-earth render coat. The intrados between the ribs are concave to enhance acoustic performance. The finishing coat contains 5 % of linseed oil varnish, so it essentially also acts as a vapour barrier.

The floor construction is particularly economical: it is comprised of recycled pallets with straw bale insulation. On top of the bales, "floating" OSB boards were installed; the joints were reinforced with 30-cm-wide OSB strips.

The building has a 1.5-m-tall base, which is enclosed by planted earthwork. The interior floor level is higher than the exterior ground level; thus, the interior base wall is only 1 m tall and was used to build a circular bench consisting of straw bales and wooden seating. The bench provides about 40 seats and gives the interior a more harmonious appearance. The exterior roof covering is formed by welded and weather-coated ultramarine polyester. The polyester membrane is fixed to the base wall with clamping-sleeves and can be stretched if required. According to the original designs, the roof is supposed to be planted with ivy.

The structure

A circular expanded concrete base supports the semi-spherical dome. The shell consists of straw bales stacked on top of radial arched rafters. At the base, the 8 x 8 cm

rafters are positioned at 55-cm centres. The bales are mounted vertically and form a 35-cm-thick thermal insulation layer. Since thermal transmission runs perpendicular to the stalks, a coefficient of heat conductivity of $\lambda = 0.045$ W/m^2 can be assumed. Plywood strips (8 mm x 8 cm) are fixed to the arches with rubber straps, compressing the straw bales. In structural terms this build-up forms a rigid composite shell, with

left II.106
below II.107, II.108

the straw bales providing horizontal stiffening. Since the timber arches have hinged bearings, two cross-laths were fixed on opposite sides to provide supplementary stiffening.

Procedures on site

An expanded concrete base wall providing excellent thermal insulation ($\lambda = 0.11$ W/m²) was built on top of the circular strip foundation. The cylindrical curb supporting the skylight and acting as a tension ring for the arched girders was installed with a special scaffolding.

The arches are hinged at the bottom and fixed to the tension ring of the upper curb. Cross-laths were fixed to provide stiffening. The straw bales were slotted between the arched girders and the plywood strips, and then fixed with the rubber straps. Only after tensioning of the entire shell were the plywood strips fixed to the upper curb. As a fire prevention measure, a coat of liquid earth slurry with rich clay content was sprayed onto both faces of the wall, so the emulsion could penetrate 2 cm into the upper straw layers.

Subsequently, the tailored roof membrane was installed and slightly prestressed with clamping-sleeves at the base wall.

The interior walls were finished with three layers of earth render, which contained expanded glass aggregate to reduce weight and was applied onto render base matting.

The intrados between the ribs are concave to spread sound. Fine-tuning to further improve the acoustic performance of the space took place after completion. (*II.102* to *II.108*)

Schematic design: Gernot Minke
Detailing: Gernot Minke, Friedemann Mahlke
Site supervision: Manfred Fahnert
Wall system: wooden shell structure with straw bale insulation
Completion: 2003
Floor area: approx. 53 m²

Farm and residential building near Rothenburg ob der Tauber, Franconia, Germany

A barn on an old farm was to be converted into a residential building. To achieve this, two thirds of the exterior walls were demolished and replaced by a post-and-beam structure consisting of laminated timber profiles (6/30 cm). The compartments were closed with straw bale infill panels. Special bales with a thickness of 30 cm were manufactured with a bale press to achieve exterior walls as thin as possible.

The supplementary structure was so skilfully integrated into the existing fabric that only two different bale lengths were required. Similarly, the ceiling height was designed to suit whole bale dimensions. This way, all exterior walls could be completed on one weekend. The exterior face of the walls received a 2.5-cm fibrous plasterboard cladding, providing the required F60 fire rating. The cladding also provides wind-tightness and structural reinforcement. A ventilated weatherboarding protects the building from the elements.

The interior faces received a 3-cm trass-lime render with an additional earth finishing coat in the living areas. In this case, the lime render was chosen to protect the bales from the moisture of the earth render.
(II.109 to II.113)

Design: Sabine Rothfuß
Site supervision: Sabine Rothfuß
Wall system: prefabricated timber post-and-beam structure with spelt straw infill panels
Completion: 2003
Living/Floor area: 310 + 80 m²

from top to bottom
II.109, II.110

from left to right
II.111, I.112

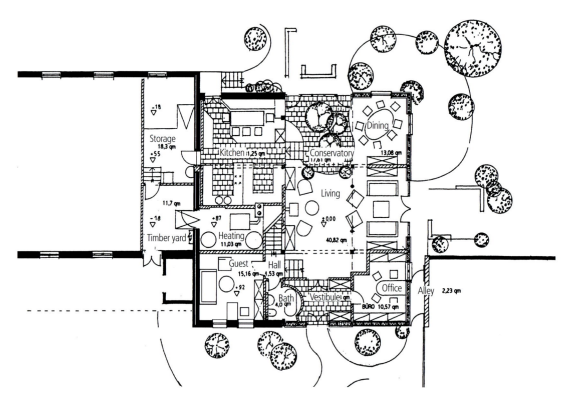

II.113

■ House of a painter near Santa Cruz, California, USA

The site of this passive solar straw bale home in the Santa Cruz Mountains is only a few miles away from the epicentre of the 1989 Loma Prieta earthquake. It replaces a smaller framed structure that actually fell off its foundation during that earthquake. In addition to post-and-beam with steel X-bracing, the wall system utilizes the lateral strength of the plastered straw bale walls.

This California bale wall system is optimised as a stressed skin panel for lateral resistance. The lime-cement plaster is reinforced with 14 ga. 2" x 2" welded wire mesh well anchored to the sill plates for tension. The wire provides a tension net to contain the compression strut of the plastered bales. The resilient compressibility of the bale provides significant ductility during seismic crushing, matching the ductility of plywood shear walls.

Designed for a painter and his family of five, the 325-m² structure features a two-story entrance hall, which also serves as an art gallery. All rooms in the house relate to the central south-facing courtyard, which offers a spectacular view of the Pacific Ocean. Many French doors and window seats in the 2-feet-thick walls create a strong connection to the outdoors. The building has been carefully situated to preserve existing redwood groves, provide wind shelter and capture the natural beauty of the surroundings in all directions.

A vaulted ceiling spans the family room, while exposed trusses support the second-floor roof. The rich texture of the exposed structural members relates to the sculptural qualities of the bale walls. Details and finishes emphasise craftsmanship, including the custom-built Rumford fireplaces that are made from salvaged brick. In keeping with local tradition, mission tile covers the main roof. Therefore, solar equipment will be installed on accessory structures. A combined solar thermal system will provide domestic hot water as well as auxiliary

above II.114
left II.115
next page II.116

space heating in the winter and pool heating in the summer, respectively.
(*II.114* to *II.116*)

Design: DSA Architects – Dan Smith, Dietmar Lorenz
Owner / Builder: Gordon Smedt
Wall system: post-and-beam construction, straw bale walls
Completion: 2005
Living / Floor area: 325 m²

■ Foothills Academy College Preparatory, Scottsdale, Arizona, USA

At the time of its completion, the Foothills private college preparatory with a size of 2,000 m² was one of the largest straw bale buildings worldwide. Buildings containing classrooms as well as a media centre and administrative offices are grouped around a central square, which is also used as an outdoor classroom.

Located at the banks of an existing riverbed, the design ensured that the natural waterways were not altered or disturbed. The scheme respects the character of the surrounding landscape and the natural vegetation. Rainwater is collected and recycled for irrigation.

The large glazed areas of the building comply with passive solar design principles and ensure sufficient solar gains during winter. Large roof overhangs prevent overheating during summer. The building's mechanical engineering such as water-saving technology and natural ventilation is likewise designed to minimise negative impact on the environment.

The building structure consists of steel and reinforced concrete columns, which are insulated with straw bales. They are connected to each other and to the roof with metal pins. The walls were rendered with cement-based and acrylic-modified stucco. (II.117 to II.122)

Design: Weddle + Gilmore Architects
Site supervision: Tom Hahn, Three Rivers EcoBuilders
Wall system: steel and reinforced concrete frame with straw bale insulation and cement-based render
Completion: 2002
Living / Floor area: 2,050 m²

from top to bottom
II.117, II.118
right II.119

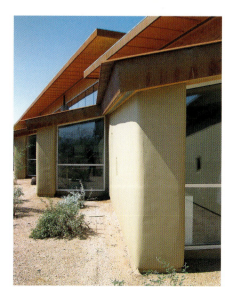

left II.121
below II.122
left page II.120

■ Real Goods Solar Living Center, Hopland, California, USA

The Solar Living Institute was founded in 1998 as a spin-off of Real Goods Trading Company – one of the United States' leading suppliers for renewable energy, energy- and water-saving and environmentally friendly consumer products.

The Institute is a non-profit organisation offering advanced training in the fields of renewable energy, alternative sustainable building and engineering methods, sustainable lifestyle and ecological design. The Solar Living Center, the building in which the Institute is housed, serves as a display of the corporate philosophy. Some 200,000 people visit the Center and the 5.6-ha site every year.

The building structure consists of a restricted number of concrete columns supporting arched laminated timber girders. Instead of Portland cement, the concrete of the columns and floors contains fly ash – pulverised cremated coal. Rear and sidewalls received rice straw infill panels. In California, rice straw is usually a waste product that is combusted: the alternative use is a real contribution to the reduction of greenhouse gas emission and provides an additional source of income for the farmers.

Thanks to the passive solar system, the building does nearly without conventional

Design: Van der Ryn Architects
Design team: David Arkin, Bruce King
Wall system: timber-concrete structure, rice straw infill panels
Completion: 1996
Floor area: approx. 460 m^2

heating and completely without cooling. During winter, the sun enters deeply into the building and during summer the large roof overhang provides shade. Additionally, the indoor climate is controlled by a ventilation system and the thermal mass of the building elements. Water fountains and a canopy with wine tendrils form a kind of solar barrier which ensures a constant indoor temperature of 22 to 26 °C without artificial cooling even on extremely hot summer days.

The straw bale walls have been rendered with gunearth (cement-enhanced earth render). The roof has been covered with a Hypalon® membrane.
The Center has a photovoltaic plant with an output of 10 kW and a wind power plant with an output of 3 kW – this covers the Center's entire energy demand. Surplus solar power can even be sold and fed back into the local grid. (*II.123* to *II.125*)

above II.125
left page from top
to bottom II.123,
II.124

II.126

II.127

International Sivananda Yoga Vedanta Center Lodge, Val-Morin, Quebec, Canada

The Sivananda Ashram Yoga Camp was founded in 1963 and is the headquarters of the International Sivananda Yoga Vedanta Centers – a Yoga style named after its founder Swami Sivananda (1887–1963). It is situated in the Laurentian Mountains north of Montreal. The 25-year-old summer guesthouse burned down in the summer of 1994. Hence, replacement was required as soon as possible to hold up guest operations.

The entire building is based on the 1.20 x 1.20 m grid for the timber structure. The compartments between posts are filled with straw bales of the same length. All interior and exterior walls consist of lime-cement-rendered straw bales. The floor slabs are made of concrete with integrated meandering heating tubes. Coloured pigments were added to both floor and exterior render to avoid additional painting; all interior wall finishes remained white. After completion, the concrete floor was treated with linseed oil and natural wax.

The overall roof area of more than 700 m² is a green roof that is mainly covered with strawberry plants.

Licensed contractors conducted all works, except for the straw bale construction. In order to avoid interference of the different trades, all straw bale works were conducted on weekends. (*II.126* to *II.128*)

II.128

Design: Archibio, Michel Bergeron
Site supervision: Archibio, Michel Bergeron
Wall system: 15/15-cm timber post-and-beam structure on 1.20 m x 1.20 m grid with straw bale infill panels
Completion: 1996
Living / Floor area: approx. 1,100 m²

Waldorf school in Carbondale, Colorado, USA

In 1996, the Roaring Fork Waldorf School decided to give up its old premises and build a new school complying with the principles of the Waldorf philosophy and consisting of healthy and natural materials on a 13-acre site.

To date, three buildings were erected – one kindergarten (approx. 315 m²), one for the first to eighth grades (approx. 530 m²) and a multi-purpose wing accommodating the auditorium, offices, and music and dance rehearsal rooms. A further building of 420 m² for the higher grades is currently at planning stage.

In addition to the use of natural materials like earth, linoleum, non-toxic colours and paints, the design ensured maximum use of solar energy. Furthermore, state-of-the-art knowledge on stimulating learning environments was incorporated into the planning process. Accordingly, every classroom faces south and comprises skylights for optimal daylighting – although in the kindergarten, skylights were not installed. Here, ceilings are also lower to give the children a greater sense of comfort and security. The straw bale insulation restricts the required heat use to a minimum of a few days during winter, which is provided by under-floor heating. The straw bales also provide excellent sound insulation so that the adjacent highway does not disturb the students at all.

All in all, building cost could be restricted to about US $ 700/m² due to the high percentage of do-it-yourself construction. (*II.129* to *II.131*)

from top to bottom
II.129, II.130

Design and site supervision: Jeff Dickinson
Wall system: timber frame with straw
bale insulation
Completion: 2000
Living/Floor area: approx. 1,870 m^2 (kindergarten, grades one to eight, and multi-purpose
building), a further 420 m^2 for the higher grades
(currently at planning stage)

from top to bottom left to right II.132, II.133, II.134, II.135, II.136, II.137

right page from top to bottom II.138, II.139

■ Salem Children's Village, Kaliningrad, Russia

North of Kaliningrad – formerly Königsberg – the first Salem Children's Village in Russia has been built. It comprises ten houses for ten to twelve homeless Russian orphans each.

A woman or couple sharing the house with them will look after these kids and youths, most of whom were collected from the street. In order to insure self-supply and provide professional training for the youths, the scheme also incorporates market gardens and a farm for organic agriculture and gardening. The village's food is strictly vegetarian, smoking is prohibited on the premises and there is no television; this regime is to create an environment enabling the children to grow up mentally and physically healthy and become integrated into society in positive way.

Salem-Rus is a German-Russian joint venture conceived as a model project for advanced nutrition, upbringing and training. The pictured building is the second to be completed on the premises. It comprises an area of 270 m², housing up to eleven children and their custodians. The building is based on an economical octagonal plan with a central multi-purpose space for eating, playing and lounging. The building's shape also minimises the area of exterior walls and therefore thermal losses. A central skylight provides sufficient daylight for the space.

The exterior walls consist of a primary timber frame with a facing straw bale wall. The exterior timber cladding is supported by secondary timber structure fixed to the primary frame, the roof and the foundation. During a two-week workshop, the walls were erected by German students and finished with earth slurry providing air-tightness and fire protection. The interior faces were partially rendered, and the timber frame compartments were filled with earth bricks. The roof was planted with wild grasses.

According to Russian building regulations, tripled windows had to be used: due to a lack of local supply, eventually double-glazed casement windows with additional single glazing were used. (*II.132* to *II.139*)

Design: Gernot Minke
Straw bale works: Gernot Minke, Friedemann Mahlke
Wall system: timber frame with straw bale infill panels
Completion: 2003
Living/Floor area: 270 m²

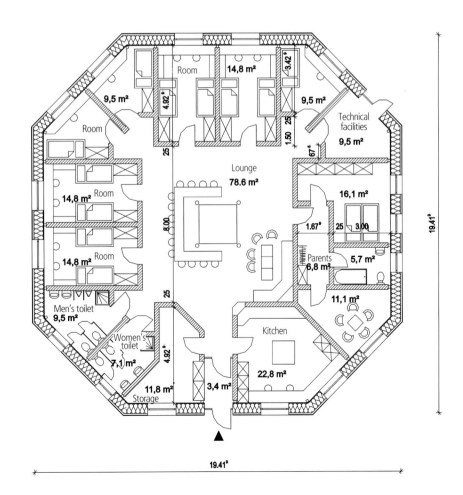

Sanctuary House, Creston, Colorado, USA

The Sanctuary House – a spiritual centre for representatives of all religions – is situated near Crestone at the foothills of the Sangre de Cristo Mountains, Colorado. Besides being a place for religious activities, the centre also offers the opportunity for advanced education in sustainable building and lifestyle. The project is to serve as a model for a simple and integrated, yet comfortable way of living. The core of the premises is a courtyard with an imitation of the maze in the gothic cathedral of Chartres. It is framed by four meditation spaces, which represent the world's four major religious traditions: Jewish/Christian, Buddhist/Zen, Hindu/Vedic and Sufi/Muslim. Three supplementary rooms for visitors complete the premises. This building as well as the owners' residence have been built with local tree trunks and insulated with straw bales.

The wall finishes and floors are made of multi-coloured local types of earth.

The roofs are insulated with 15-cm styrofoam and received a metal cladding. Heating and cooling energy use is reduced to minimum by the orientation of windows – large ones facing south and small window openings facing north. (*II.140* to *II.141*)

from top to bottom
II.140, II.141

Design: Touson Saryon, Integral Design Studio
Site supervision and wall construction:
Paul Koppana
Wall system: timber-framed structure out of roundwood with straw bale insulation
Completion: 2003
Living/Floor area: approx. 187 m² (residential building)

■ Vipassana Meditation Hall, Blackheath, Australia

At the Vipassana Meditation Centre in Blackheath, Australia, Vipassana meditation is taught and practiced in courses of several days each. Vipassana – which in free translation means "to see things as they really are" – is one of the oldest meditation techniques in India. It focuses on the ability to overcome inner unrest following certain rules. Courses are exclusively financed through donations, in most cases donations that were made by participants of preceding courses. The centre is the oldest of its kind in Australia and so far only the second outside of India. The building is situated on a 16-ha site in the Blue Mountains, New South Wales.

The meditation building essentially consists of a large meditation space with two separate foyer spaces for men and women in front and a small Dharma hall in between. The building consists of a load-bearing steel structure with straw bale infill panels that were rendered with earth. The façade is protected from rain by a 1.2-m-wide veranda. The straw bale walls are 3 m and 4.2 m tall, respectively, and – due to their height – were reinforced with external bamboo pinning. Pressed straw boards form part of the ceiling and provide excellent sound insulation. Heating for the meditation room is provided by under-floor heating driven by solar energy (*II.142* to *II.143*).

II.142

Design: David Baggs
Straw bale works: Frank Thomas
Wall system: steel post-and-beam structure with straw bale infill panels
Completion: 2002
Living / Floor area: 450 m²

II.143

Measures

In this book, all measures as regards lengths and areas as well as physical values are based on the metric system. The Angle-Saxon equivalent of the U-value (describing thermal conductivity in Central Europe) is the R-value, which has been added in brackets. In this context, it must be noted that the R-values are based on the metric system.

To enable readers to convert values into the imperial system that is most commonly used in North America we have listed the most important conversion factors as follows:

Lengths and areas

1 mm = 0.03937 inches
1 cm = 0.3937 inches
1 m = 39.37 inches

1 m^2 = 10.764 square feet
1 ha = 2.471 acres

1 inch = 2.54 cm
1 foot = 30.48 cm

1 square foot = 0.093 m^2
1 acre = 0.4047 ha

Physical values

Temperature
Centigrade (Celsius) – Fahrenheit
Multiply by 9/5 and add 32

°C	°F
– 10	14
0	32
10	50
20	68
30	86

R- and U-values

All R- and U-values in this book have been stated according to the metric system. For the conversion of the metric system (USI, RSI) into the respective imperial system (U, R), the use of factors is required:

R x 0.1761= RSI
RSI x 5.6783 = R

U-values are the reciprocals of the respective R-values and vice versa.

USI (W/m^{2}K)	RSI (m^{2}K/W)	U (BTU/hr * sq. ft. * °F)	R (hr * sq. ft. * °F/BTU)
0.1	10	0.018	56.78
0.15	6.667	0.026	37.86
0.2	5	0.035	20.39
0.3	3.333	0.053	18.93
0.5	2	0.080	11.36
1.0	1	0.176	5.68

Networks

To the present day, the proliferation of straw bale building mainly relies on the cooperation of national and international networks. They are an information pool for the exchange of technical knowledge, and the launching of campaigns – for instance for the official approval of straw bales as building material – here often takes its origin. An industrial lobby advocating its own commercial interests is not – or only to a very small degree – involved in straw bale building. Thus, all information is freely accessible. On the other hand, precisely because of its independent character, straw bale building relies on the voluntary participation of many people, which can slow down certain procedures. Following, we have compiled a brief list of various networks – this list, however, does not claim to be complete.

Global Straw Building Network GSBN
GSBN is a network of organisations promoting and using technology related to straw bale building and straw-based materials. It handles the coordination of research projects and events, the proliferation of documentations as well as communication between the local networks. In order to restrict the number of participants to a manageable level, only representatives of straw bale organisations and straw bale experts can join up.

Europäisches Strohballennetzwerk ESBN
The first ESBN (European Straw Bale Network) meeting took place in 1998 in France. On the second meeting in Denmark, national networks for instance for England, Denmark, the Netherlands, France and Austria were founded. These meetings take place annually or every other year. In the meantime, an English mailing list ensures lively exchange of information.
http://amper.ped.muni.cz/mailman/listinfo/strawbale

California Straw Building Association CASBA
This is an important US network consisting of architects, engineers, straw bale builders and educated laypersons. CASBA aims at the proliferation and development of knowledge on straw bale building through research and education.
http://www.strawbuilding.org

The Straw Bale Building Association SBBA (WISE)
Straw bale network of Wales, Ireland, Scotland and England, coordinating cooperation between these countries.
http://www.strawbalebuildingassociation.org.uk

Fachverband Strohballenbau Deutschland e.V. FSB
The FSB is committed to the open and cooperative exchange between straw bale builders. The association strives to make access to information related to straw bale building public – and to keep it this way – so that straw bale building and planning anywhere in Germany will not be restricted by private licences and patents. The association is non-profit as a rule – all research data should be provided free of charge. The research on thermal conductivity and the two successfully passed fire tests mentioned in this book are first fruits of FSB's work.
http://www.fasba.de

Österreichisches Strohballen-Netzwerk asbn
The Austrian straw bale network defines itself as a platform providing information to people interested in straw bale building. It is to be an interface between private clients who wish to build with straw bales, and planners and builders. One can subscribe to a regularly updated newsletter by e-mail. The network is maintained and presented by Astrid and Herbert Gruber. The respective website contains a large and well-edited information base on the topic as well as image galleries on straw bale buildings from all over the world.
http://www.baubiologie.at/asbn.htm

Internet links

General note

The Internet has been pivotal in the proliferation of straw bale building. It has been a platform for chat groups and exchange of know-how that was, and continues to be, accessible to everyone who is interested. For this reason, we have added a selection of interesting links about straw bale building. Further links can be easily detected via the usual search engines.

Due to the fast-moving nature of the Internet, some of the links listed below may not be updated any more or have been removed altogether. Therefore, the authors have provided the same link list on their own webpage under http://www.uni-kassel.de/fb6/minke; this will save the reader the hassle of faulty connections; furthermore, here links are regularly updated, added or replaced. Please note as well that some pages are best viewed with the newest browser versions.

General link lists

Burbophobia
Links on straw bale building and other sustainability-related topics.
http://moxvox.com/straw.html

Surfin' StrawBale
Largest existing link compilation on straw bale building.
http://mha-net.org/html/sblinks.htm

Amazon Nails
Homepage of Barbara Jones' company Amazon Nails.
http://www.strawbalefutures.org.uk

ASBN – Austrian straw bale network
Largest German-language site with extensive information, galleries and downloads.
http://www.baubiologie.at/asbn.htm

Balewatch
Includes 50, sometimes imaginative, floor plans of different sizes mainly aiming at the American market.
http://www.balewatch.com

Building Codes
General page by DCAT on building regulations and planning with relevant links.
http://www.azstarnet.com/~dcat/codes.htm

CASBA – California Straw Building Association
Major institution in the field of straw bale building.
http://www.strawbuilding.org

Chug's World of Straw Bale Building
Information and images from the UK.
http://www.strawbale-building.co.uk

ESBN – Mailingliste
Chat forum of the European Straw Bale Network.
http://amper.ped.muni.cz/mailman/listinfo/strawbale

Fachverband Strohballenbau Deutschland e.V.
German community of designers, builders and private parties committed to the proliferation of straw bale building in Germany and promoting official research to facilitate planning procedures for such projects.
http://www.fasba.de

International Straw Bale Building Registry
Project committed to the registration of straw bale buildings worldwide, large data pool on the buildings.
http://sbregistry.greenbuilder.com

Out on Bale
Homepage of Matts Myhrman and Judy Knox, the straw bale building pioneers.
http://www.azstarnet.com/~dcat/outbale.htm

Pilot Study of Moisture Control in Stuccoed Straw Bale Walls
Study on moisture control of straw bales.
http://www.cmhc-schl.gc.ca/en/imquaf/hehosu/stbawa/stbawa_001.cfm

Strobouw Nederland
Homepage on the topic by Rene Dalmeijer, one of the best-known international networkers.
http://home.hetnet.nl/~rene.dalmeijer

The Last Straw
Homepage of quarterly magazine The Last Straw.
http://www.strawhomes.com

The Straw Bale Building Association
Homepage of the British Straw Bale Building Association with information, events and picture galleries.
http://www.strawbalebuildingassociation.org.uk

The Thermal Resistivity of Straw Bales for Construction
Research by J. McCabe on the issue of thermal conductivity.
http://sol.crest.org/efficiency/straw_insulation/straw_insul.html

Design practices and contractors dealing in straw bale building

Archibio
Ontario, Canada. Michel Bergeron. Architect and straw bale builder.
http://www.archibio.qc.ca

Camel's Back Construction
Ontario, Canada. Chris Magwood, Pete Mack, Tina Therrien. Design and construction.
http://www.strawhomes.ca

DSA Architects
California, USA. Dietmar Lorenz, Daniel Smith. Architectural practice, design and realisation of straw bale buildings.
http://www.dsaarch.com

One World Design
Washington State, USA. Kelly Lerner. Architectural practice, design and realisation of straw bale buildings.
http://www.one-world-design.com

Yesterday-Today-Tomorrow/Strawbale Construction
Australia. Frank Thomas, Paul Dowling. Design of straw bale buildings and realisation of straw bale and finishing works as well as interior fit-out.
http://www.strawbale.com.au

Further links

Builders without Borders
International network of sustainable designers with a focus on straw bale and earth building.
http://www.builderswithoutborders.org

CREST – Renewable Energy Policy Project
Homepage on renewable energy; at http://www.crest.org/discussion/strawbale/200201/ chat forum on straw bale building.
http://www.crest.org/index.html

DCAT – Development Center for Appropriate Technology
David Eisenberg – comprehensive link on sustainability including straw bale building.
http://www.dcat.net

Ecological Building Network
By Bruce King, building material researcher and straw bale builder. King founded an international network on sustainable building.
http://www.ecobuildnetwork.org

Natural Building Resources
Book and video bank, hosted by Catherine Wanek.
http://www.strawbalecentral.com

Selected homepages on featured projects

Sabine Rothfuß, rehabilitation of agricultural premises
http://www.architektur-con-terra.de/Aktuell.html

Julia Bourke, residential building in central Montreal
http://www.mchg.mcgill.ca/bourke/Mardivert_pres/index.htm

Singe-family home in Dobersdorf, Burgenland, Austria
http://strohballenhaus.port5.com

Real Goods Solar Living Center, Hopland, California, USA
http://www.solarliving.org
http://www.realgoods.com

Residential building in Ouwerkerk, Zeeland, the Netherlands
http://home.concepts-ict.nl/~rened/houses/sbnl.html

Trout Farm Complex, Tassaraja Canyon, California, USA
http://www.slosustainability.com

First straw bale house in Vienna, Austria
http://www.allmermacke.at

Low-energy house in Maria Laach, Austria
http://www.bauatelier.at/niedrigenergiehaus2.html

Passive house, Cavan, Ontario, Canada
http://www.glenhunter.ca/

Residential and office building, London, United Kingdom
http://www.thebankofideas.org/s_projects.html

Sanctuary House, Crestone, Colorado, USA
http://www.sanctuaryhouse.org

House of a painter near Santa Cruz, California, USA
http://www.dsaarch.com/galery_house.htm

Urban cottage in Berkeley, California, USA
http://www.dsaarch.com/bekeley%20cottage.htm

Bibliography

Amazon Nails: *Information Guide to Straw Bale Building*, Todmorden, UK, 2001.

Bauer et al.: "Nachwachsende Rohstoffe im Bauwesen", in: *Gesundheits-Ingenieur*, 2000/Vol. 3.

Boenkendorf, U.; Knöfel, D.: "Les Mortiers d'Enduit dans la Construction en Pan de Bois," in: *Proceedings of the International Congress on the Conservation of Stone and Other Materials*, Unesco/Rilem, Paris, 29 June–1 July 1993

Brown, G.Z., et al.: *Moisture in a Strawbale Wall*, University of Oregon, 1998, p. 14

Bühring, J.: "Putz und Farbe an Fachwerkbauten," in: *Arbeitsgemeinschaft Historische Fachwerkstädte in Hessen und Niedersachsen*, Ed.: Arbeitsgruppe Bautechnik, Vol. 3, no date.

Canadian Society of Agricultural Engineering: *Thermal and Mechanical Properties of Straw Bales as They Relate to a Straw House*, Ottawa, Ontario, Canada, 1995

Doolittle, B.: "A Round House of Straw Bales," *Mother Earth News* 19/1973: pp. 52-57

Eweleit, Sven; Hansen, Lorenz; Meinhof, Sven: *Strohballen – Bauen für eine bessere Zukunft*, Forschungsbericht an der Universität Hannover, 1999

FEB (Forschungslabor für Experimentelles Bauen), Universität Kassel: *Bestimmung der Wärmeleitfähigkeit von Strohballen*, 2000 (unpublished report)

Feist, W: *Grundlagen der Gestaltung von Passivhäusern*, Darmstadt, 1996

Fernandez, Manuel A.: *Two-Hour Fire Testing on Straw Bales*, Constr. Industries Comm. of New Mexico, Santa Fe, New Mexico, USA, 1993

Gagné, Louis: *Strawbale Demonstration Project*, Canada Mortage & Housing Comp., Ottawa, Ontario, Canada, 1986

Gammelin, T.: *Strohballenhäuser als Unterkunft für Betroffene von Naturkatastrophen und Migration*, Master's thesis, FH Würzburg – Schweinfurt, 2002

Gerner, M.: *Farbiges Fachwerk*, Stuttgart 1983

Goodwin, B.: "Winery Builds Country's Biggest," in: Gray, A. T.; Hall, A. (Eds.) *Strawbale Homebuilding*, Treutham, Victoria, Australia, 2000

Götte, K.: *Feuchtmeßtechnik*, Berlin, 1966

GrAT: *Haus der Zukunft*, study commissioned by the Austrian Federal Ministry of Transport, Innovation and Technology in cooperation with asbn and StrohTec, Vienna, 2001 (b)

GrAT: *Wandsysteme aus nachwachsenden Rohstoffen*, fundamental study relating to economic aspects, final report, Vienna, 2001 (a)

GrAT: *Planen und Bauen für die Zukunft – Das S-House*, Vienna, 2002

Gray, A.T.; Hall, A. (Eds.): *Strawbale Homebuilding*, Treutham, Victoria, Australia, 2000

Gruber, Astrid; Gruber, Herbert: *Bauen mit Stroh*, Ökobuch-Verlag, Staufen, 2000

Huff 'n' Puff Construction: *Pre-Compressed Straw Bale Walls* (report); Kangaroo Valley, NSW, Australia

Jolly, Rob; commissioned by CMHC (Canada Mortgage and Housing Corp.): *Strawbale Moisture Monitoring Report*, 2000

Kemble, Steven: *How to Build Your Elegant Home with Straw Bales – Manual: A Guide for the Owner Builder*, Version 1.0, Bisbee, AZ, 1995

King, Bruce: *Buildings of Earth and Straw – Structural Design for Rammed Earth and Straw Bale Architecture*, Sausalito, California, USA, 1996

Lacinski, Paul; Bergeron, Michel: *Serious Straw Bale – A Home Construction Guide for all Climates*, Chelsea Green Publishing, Vermont/Totnes, 2000

Leszner, T.; Stein, J.: *Lehm-Fachwerk*, Köln 1987

Mac Donald, S.O.: *A Visual Primer to Straw-Bale Construction in Mongolia*, Gila, New Mexico, USA, 1999 (Appropriate Development Project)

MacDonald, S.O.; Myhrman, Matts: *Build it with Bales – A Step-by-Step Guide to Straw Bale Construction*, Version 1.0, Tucson, AZ, 1994

Magwood, Chris; Mack, Peter: *Straw Bale Building*, New Society Publishers, Gabriola Island, British Columbia, 2000

McCabe, Joseph: *The Thermal Resistivity of Straw Bales for Construction*, Master's thesis, University of Arizona, 1993

McElderry, W. & C.: "Happiness is a Hay House," *Mother Earth News* 58/1979: pp. 40-43

Minke, Gernot: *Das Neue Lehmbau-Handbuch*, Ökobuch-Verlag, Staufen, 6th edition, 2004

Minke, Gernot: *Earth Construction Handbook – The Building Material Earth in Modern Architecture*, Southhampton, 2000

National Research Council of Canada: *ASTM FireTesting on Straw Bales*, Ottawa, Ontario, Canada

Oehlmann, M.: "Die Geschichte des Strohballenbaus," in: Wedig, H. (Ed.) *Bauen mit Ballen*, Xanten, 1999

Pfleiderer, J.: *Bauen mit Ballen aus Stroh: Kritische Hinterfragung eines neuen/alten Baustoffes*, Master's thesis, Hildesheim, 2000

Scharmer, D.: "Ein Haus aus Stroh," in: *Wohnung und Gesundheit*, 12/2002: pp. 8-9

SHB Agra Inc. (Ed): *Report on the Full Scale Wall Assembly Load Test, Transverse Load Test Small Scale E-119 Fire Test on Uncoated Straw Bale Wall Panels and Stucco Coated Straw Bale Wall Panels*, Albuquerque, New Mexico, USA, 1993

Steen, Athena; Steen, Bill: *The Beauty of Straw Bale Homes*, Chelsea Green Publishing, Vermont/Totnes, 2000

Steen, Athena; Steen, Bill; Bainbridge, David; Eisenberg, David: *The Straw Bale House*, Chelsea Green Publishing, Vermont/Totnes, 1994

Strang, G.: "Straw Bale Studio," *Fine Homebuilding*, 12/1983: pp. 70-72

Straube, J.: *Moisture Properties of Plaster and Stucco for Strawbale Buildings*, Canada Mortgage and Housing Corp., Canada, June 2000

Unger, Josef: *Stroh als Baustoff, zu schade zum Verheizen*, conference papers, Illmitz, 2001

Viitanen, Hannu: *Factors Affecting the Development of Mould and Brown Rot Decay in Wooden Material and Wooden Structures*, Uppsala University, 1996, sec. 2, p. 25

Wanek, Catherine (Ed.): *The Last Straw: The Grassroots Journal of Straw-Bale and Natural Building*, Hillboro, New Mexico, USA

Wanek, Catherine: *The New Straw Bale Home*, Layton, Utah, 2003

Wedig, Harald (Ed.): *Bauen mit Ballen*, Xanten 1999

Wedig, Harald: "GUS-Staaten," in: *Stroh im Kopf*, 1/1999: p. 7

Wehlte, K.: *Werkstoffe und Techniken der Malerei*, Ravensburg, 5th edition, 1985

Weiß, A.: *Angewandte Chemie* 75/1963: pp. 755-762

Welsch, R.L.: "Sandhill Baled-Hay Construction," *Keystone Folklore Quarterly*, Spring Issue 1970: pp. 16-34

Welsch, R.L.: "Baled Hay," in: *Shelter* (L. Kahn, ed.), p. 70, Shelter Publications, Bolinas, California, 1973

Wingate-Pearse, Susan; Glassford, John: "The Wizard of Oz," in: *The Last Straw*, 24/1998: p. 17

Wisser, S.; Knöfel, D.: "Untersuchungen zu historischen Putz- und Mauermörteln," in: *Bautenschutz und Bausanierung*, 5/1988: pp. 163–171

Acknowledgements

We would like to extend our thanks to all who have contributed to this book with their suggestions and critique but also by granting vital material – above all to Karen Allmer and Florian Macke, Michel Bergeron, Matthias and Ruth Bönisch, Julia Bourke, Rolf Brinkmann, Rene Dalmeijer, David Eisenberg, John Glassford, Herbert Gruber, Tom Hahn, Glen Hunter, Hertha Hurnaus, Bruce King, Axel Linde, Chris Magwood, Frank Millies, Katsura Nakano, Martin Oehlmann. Special thanks go to Dirk Scharmer, Lüneburg, for his numerous suggestions and his guidance in the fields of building material testing and planning permissions, and for the provision of comprehensive imagery; to Frank Thomas and Ingrid Leusch, Moss Vale, Australia, for their support during various site visits in Australia, the provision of images and detailed drawings of their work, and the proof-reading of the English translation; and to Dietmar Lorenz, Winfried Schmelz and Catherine Wanek for the provision of comprehensive imagery and information.

Illustration credits

Allmer, Karen: *II.64, II.66*
Barnes, Richard: *II.123–125*
Berg, Arild: *2.13*
Bergeron, Michel: *3.1, 4.6, II.9, II.12–13, II.126–128*
Blöchl, Wolfgang: *7.8, 9.12*
Bourke, Julia: *II.10–11*
de Bouter, Andre: *2.5*
Bramm, Ulrich: *2.14*
Eisenberg, David: *2.1, 2.2, 2.4, 2.7*
Dalmeijer, Rene: *2.12, II.51–53*
Fahnert, Manfred: *II.102*
FEB: *10.2, 10.3–5*
Fischer, Alexander: *5.8*
Glassford, John: *2.19*
GrAT: *4.1, 4.2*
Gruber, Herbert: *II.14–21*
Hahn, Tom: *II.117–122*
Harbusch, Gerald: *II.22–26*
Henselmans, Jan: *2.6*
Hunter, Glen: *II.59–62*
Hurnaus, Hertha: *II.63, II.65, II.67*
Huth, Klaus: *II.90–92*
Jones, Barbara: *II.54*
Kennedy, Declan: *2.12*
The Last Straw: *2.8*
Lautenbach, Katja: *7.27–7.29*
Linde, Axel: *II.94–96*
Lipfert, Gerhard: *II.138*
Lorenz, Dietmar: *II.27–31, II.114–116*
Macke, Florian: *II.64, II.66*
Mahlke, Friedemann: *1.1–4, 2.16–17, 4.7, 4.8, 5.1–5, 5.6–8, 6.2–7, 6.8–10, 6.13, 6.14, 7.1–2, 7.7, 7.9–10, 7.11–14, 7.15–18, 7.21–22, 7.23–26, 7.30–41, 7.42–43, 7.44, 7.45, 7.47, 8.2, 8.3, 8.8, 9.5, 9.8–9, II.1–6, II.39, II.68–70, II.97–101, II.102–103, II.105, II.107–108*
Millies, Frank: *3.3, 6.11, 9.1, 9.3, 9.6–7*
Minke, Gernot: *2.15, 6.12, 7.3–6, 7.46, 8.1, 8.7, 9.2–4, 9.10–11, 9.13–19, 10.1, 10.6–30, II.7–8, II.104, II.106, II.132–137*
Oehlmann, Martin: *2.9, 2.11*
Nakano, Katsura: *II.44–50*
Rothfuß, Sabine: *II.109–113*
San Luis Sustainability Group: *II.78–82*
Scharmer, Dirk: *2.18–19, 3.2, II.93*
Schmelz, Winfried: *II.71–74, II.75–77*
Schmidt, Werner: *II.55–58*
Smoothy, Paul: cover photograph, *II.83–89*
Steen, Bill: *2.3, 4.3, 4.4–5, 7.19, 8.6*
Thomas, Frank: *II.36–38, II.142–143*
Wanek, Catherine: *II.40–43, II.129–131, II.140–141*
Williams, Nick: *II.32–35*

Graphic design: Gabrielle Pfaff, Berlin
Translation: Jörn Frenzel, Berlin

A CIP catalogue record for this book is available
from the Library of Congress, Washington D.C.,
USA

Bibliographic information published by
Die Deutsche Bibliothek
Die Deutsche Bibliothek lists this publication in the
Deutsche Nationalbibliografie; detailed biblio-
graphic data is available in the internet at
<http://dnb.ddb.de>.

© 2005 Birkhäuser – Publishers for Architecture,
P.O. Box 133, CH-4010 Basel, Switzerland
for the revised and enlarged English edition
Part of Springer Science+Business Media
Printed on acid-free paper produced
from chlorine-free pulp. TCF ∞

Originally published in German under the title of
"Der Strohballenbau: Ein Konstruktionshandbuch"
Copyright © 2004 ökobuch Verlag GmbH,
Staufen bei Freiburg/Breisgau
All rights reserved.

Printed in Germany
ISBN 3-7643-7171-4

9 8 7 6 5 4 3 2 1   http://www.birkhauser.ch

Front cover: part of a residential and office building in London, United Kingdom